The 5 Pillars of Positive Thinking

Master Your Mind

Proven Strategies to Cultivate Joy, Confidence, and Inner Peace.
Control Your Thoughts and Unleash Your True Potential for
Happiness and Success

DAVID HEIMBACHER

Table of Contents

Foreword

Time and time again, people feel the need to change their lives from the ground up. Do you also feel the need to do so? Then you will quickly notice that there are many hurdles in implementing change. The body, the mind - your entire self resists change. Take a look back at your past: How often have you made new resolutions at the turn of each year and then discarded them after a short time? You are not alone in this: according to scientific estimates, around 80 percent of all New Year's resolutions fail. Change is a great challenge with a high failure rate at all levels.

Maintaining our focus on the great opportunities that change represents is hard. This pattern is deeply embedded in us that the desire for new habits is always accompanied by fear: the fear of failure. It severely hinders us from implementing the behavior that we long for. In the beginning, we pour out an incredible amount of energy, which we lack when permanently integrating new habits into our lives.

This book dispels the myth that change - whether on a personal or professional level - is always difficult. Fortunately, soon you will become one of those people who focus on their goals and succeed - thanks to proven methods - in establishing new habits permanently in your own life with ease. We will focus on individual training that helps you personally and in all areas of your life to make your desired changes a reality.

This book starts with your inner self: you will learn how to strengthen your mind and make room for positive thoughts. In addition, a healthy mind needs a healthy vessel, which is why you'll also learn about various influencing factors that give you physical strength and, thus, mental strength. You will work purposefully with the valuable information through which you will develop into a disciplined and improved self: Define firm goals and integrate new habits easily with the Japanese method of success: Kaizen.

Now is your chance to finally overcome your inner hurdles and change your life. Realize how easy it is to put the change you are longing for into action!

How to Strengthen Your Mind

Surrounded by stress at work and in your personal life, your entire self becomes powerless over time. Your mind reaches its limits from being overworked. Again and again, your inner voice points out to you that something in your life is fundamentally problematic: you need rest. The same inner voice has probably urged you to get this book and study the subject of self-healing. Every master knows that the teacher appears when the student is ready. Finally, this book allows you to grow into an improved version of yourself.

You are still trapped in a habitual negative thinking pattern that puts a gloomy film on your life and every event, no matter how wonderful, if only for the simple reason that you are forever looking back and thus unhappy in the present. But there is a way out of this vicious circle, which is relatively simple at its core. Of course, it involves the fervent desire to change something and the discipline to strive and persevere through the process - but more on that later.

We'll start with a simple metaphor that illustrates how important it is to nurture your soul: Think of your mind as your garden. If you clutter it with worries, fears, sadness, and a wistful look at the past, it will deteriorate, and the weeds will start to grow. If, on the other hand, you nourish it with positive thoughts, beautiful moments, and the insight that every setback holds something good, and if you regularly rid it of the weeds - your negative thoughts - and protect it with all your will, then it will begin to blossom in full splendor and beauty. When you free yourself from the burden of your negative thoughts, you will simplify your perception of the world.

Believe in yourself and your mental fortitude! We begin by cleaning your mind to ensure that your garden blooms in full splendor. To do this, you must first envision how wonderful your life will be if you strengthen your mind and free it of negative thoughts. Then, it's on to practice: you'll learn valuable exercises and methods for working on your mind - because it's the only thing you have complete control over, even if you've already had setbacks.

Personal Happiness Through a Healthy Mind

"The happiness of your life depends upon the quality of your thoughts."

Marcus Aurelius, a Roman Emperor and Philosopher in the second century AD, once quoted this. Even back then, he recognized how people could find happiness: by focusing on the positive aspects of life.

People are all the same deep inside despite their individual and beautiful idiosyncrasies. Nevertheless, two types of people differ in their way of thinking: the pessimist and the optimist. The pessimist likes to call himself a realist, although he lives relatively far from reality because he categorically ignores positive things. Almost pathologically, he clings to setbacks. Looking into the past, which is always better than his stressful present, he loses joy. He keeps himself in chains and interprets various events in the most negative way possible. There is a good reason for this – how he has always done it is in the power of habit. A thought pattern has become so entrenched in his mind that it paralyzes him and obscures his perception, making him blind to the beautiful, simple, and small things in life. The person caught up in a negative thought pattern daily robs himself of his life force. He ages. Thus, unhappy people often suffer from psychosomatic diseases. They feel physical pain that has its origin in the psyche. Science has also approached the influence of positive thoughts on physical health in a study. The result? Around 6 out of 10 people in Germany perceive their life as stressful. Time pressure, stress, the desire for more, the flood of information, and constant accessibility mean that our lives are moving faster and faster. We are losing our sense of time and have stopped valuing it. Likewise, today's myriad of options means we can no longer focus on what's important. It is vital to escape from stress and thereby gain space. Only through this will you begin to realize what truly matters in your life. You are not alone in this. This book reveals excellent methods to help you maintain your focus.

These methods help even the most pessimistic and severely over-strained person to find a way out. For this, however, one must agree to make a small sacrifice: Time. If you compare this with the time he spent walking blindly and unhappily through his life and how much time he sacrificed, the result is minimal. According to studies, people who are stressed and unhappy live shorter lives than those who clear their minds of negative thoughts. So by working with your mind, you immediately give yourself valuable time, which you may fill with positive thoughts and beautiful moments.

Next, let us contrast the pessimist with the optimist. The optimist is open to the beauty of things. He differs from the pessimist only in how he interprets and processes his circumstances. The optimist adjusts positively to the world and allows for new, inspiring thoughts rather than harboring the same negative, frustrating thoughts every day. He has taken control of his mind and stopped dividing events into positive and negative. Instead, he views his entire life as a lesson. Thus, every experience - even failure - has something good in it if only he looks for it long enough. Even in failure, the optimist can gain valuable insights. He sees a chance to grow from everything and everywhere; even the hardest struggle strengthens, and every pain is a teacher. Thus, he can consciously control his reactions and free himself from the chains of the past. The optimist revels from the thought of achieving great things, enabling himself to master seemingly insurmountable limits easily. At the same time, he is always aware that he may only enter situations in which he is self-determined. Of course, he sometimes takes on a task that does not entirely fulfill him. Nevertheless, he is satisfied with his work and senses when it starts to drain his strength so that he can free himself from it when his mind becomes severely stressed. This is an essential criterion because you spend a lot of time at work and need opportunities to develop yourself, grow, and not be overwhelmed so that your mind is clear. After all, everything created in the outside world and becomes visible to others has its origin inside: in the mind. The optimist's mindset also causes them to interpret their health as positive, increasing their happiness and success. Happy people, according to studies, live a few years longer. Studies also showed that the life expectancy of positive people at the age of 20 was higher than that of unhappy people. Likewise, older people who considered themselves happy lived an average of 7 to 8 years longer.

As a result, positive mental conditioning is required for a long, fulfilling, and successful life. If negative thoughts are taking over your mind, it often helps to question them and thus move away from your negative thought structures as much as possible. An objective look from a person you trust is a miracle cure if you want to free yourself from a downward mental spiral. Start recognizing your limitations – you don't have to have all the knowledge, any material possessions, or all the money to do this. A human being is free to choose what they want to achieve, own, or know about. Because of digitalization, information has flooded today's world dramatically. Recognizing your limitations allows you to accept the fact that you don't have to be able to do, have, or know everything.

Furthermore, it has been demonstrated that ending all situations with a positive event works wonders, as this also remains positive in the memory and creates space for well-meaning thoughts. So instead of looking back with regret, remember it as a beautiful moment and be grateful that you were able to experience it.

Would you like to work with your mind first, then with your body and your entire self? Rejoice because a beautiful, bright, and promising future awaits you! You will gain control over your life and begin to determine your destiny. Move away from the idea that material possessions are the embodiment of happiness – otherwise, you risk letting your work rob you of your soul. You should realize that you have the potential to embody happiness. To do this, you must learn mind control techniques and devote time to working on yourself; you are the best investment you will ever make. Consider all the time in the world, all the lessons, nature, and your mind to be a gift. You are more than the sum of your experiences and the circumstances that have brought you to this point. Be thankful for your perseverance and the events that brought you here. Now is your chance to capitalize on it.

You benefit in different ways:

- Your life improves on a professional, personal, and spiritual level.

- The fresh wind clears your mind and fills it with new energy.

- You learn to listen to your inner voice – your intuition.

- You broaden your perspective to see the beauty in the smallest details. In the future, you will perceive the world with greater simplicity.

- You reinterpret every mistake and every setback into a lesson, something extraordinary: a chance to grow into an improved version of yourself.

- Suddenly, new ways and means of turning your goals into reality open up to you.

- Your body will also thank you for your newfound positive radiance, making you appear younger and more vital.

- They fill your mind with new insights: the meaning of your life.

- You develop into a creative person who can find a solution to any problem, no matter how hopeless it appears.

- They discover themselves and recognize that every human has the potential for perfection.

- Your environment will also thank you because you can only care for it if you are at peace with yourself.

- Because you have control over your thoughts, you can easily eliminate bad habits and integrate new, good practices into your life.

- You require less time for any tasks because you work more efficiently. Your mind is free and open to the world. It continues to blossom with its future challenges.

- You break free from mental chains, allowing you to pursue and carry out bigger goals and plans.

Every person has the potential to free their mind, make all these profits a reality in their life and feel themselves anew. There are more benefits to this. However, first and foremost, it is about you gaining a little insight and realizing how essential it is to work with your mind.

Many people have failed to improve themselves because they focus mainly on external appearance and material factors. The body had to function and conform to the ideals of society. In doing so, the person has locked their mind into a pattern that creates negative thoughts. The person is full of self-doubt and only concerned with appearing like a successful person on the outside, yet, success on the outside - even their most significant professional advancement - is not a success unless it is equally achieved on the inside. While inner success can lead to external success, the reverse is impossible. It is a matter of training the mind to be constantly mindful, to bring everything - mind, body, and spirit - into harmony, and to discover oneself.

Free yourself from the competitive mindset most likely imprinted on you since birth. A person is constantly compared to an ideal: at school, in studies, at work, and, most likely, in the social environment. He quickly loses touch with his inner voice, which tells him what he needs. Finally, learn to let go of toxic competitive thinking and celebrate your successes independently of others.

How to Free Yourself from Negative Thoughts

Negative thoughts paralyze you to an immense extent in your everyday life. You disturb your inner peace and rob yourself of your quality of life. The impact on your entire life begins when you lose trust in yourself, interpret situations negatively, and reflect on yourself and your experiences in a way that permanently calls your identity into question.

We, humans, are social beings and are extremely dependent on interpersonal contact. A lonely life fosters a negative mindset: no one reassures us when we reach our limits, and there is no way to unload ballast or be brought back down to earth. Since your birth, your environment has had an impact on the development of your personality. Of course, it is critical to make your person as independent of external influences as possible to maintain long-term stability. Nonetheless, social contacts are priceless. In any conversation, you have the opportunity to express yourself. In a way, you are also communicating with yourself. Both physics and psychology teach us that the more hands that carry a load, the lighter it becomes.

However, the heaviness of a load is also determined by your inner attitude, for example, as a result of luck. In general, both factors are highly interdependent. A negative, pessimistic outlook encourages self-isolation, reinforcing a negative thought pattern: we feel that isolation validates our assessment of our circumstances. As a result, you must first make room for positive thoughts. This immediately positively affects your surroundings, who will perceive you as having a pleasant personality.

Your happiness is directly related to the joy of those around you. Choose your happiness carefully to avoid being influenced by the negative thoughts of others. This is not to say that you will never be able to complain or be sad again, just as a friend will occasionally turn to you for a strong shoulder and protection. As a result, you and those around you should be open to new ideas. Accept your loved ones' help and advice, and appreciate the time they spend with you. In the end, you must decide whether to follow the advice of your friends or family. Take the time to reflect on your perspective, referring back to the wise words of those around you. Reframe your thoughts positively! Rather than being angry that a rose has thorns, it seems much more pleasant to rejoice that roses bloom on a thorny bush. It's just as important to figure out how to deal with setbacks. A key statement of Buddhism is: Every life is also suffering. We have to find our way of dealing with it and grow beyond it. Even the most difficult and painful strokes of fate hold a lesson for life.

Philosophy has been concerned with the pursuit of personal happiness since ancient times: Is it the motivator of all human action? Every day, we plague ourselves with enormous efforts, hard work, and the desire to be recognized. We are led astray by the myth that recognition from others and material possessions will make us happy. We have stopped listening to our instincts, listening within ourselves, and recognizing what we truly require to be happy. Consider the future when you are on your deathbed: Does it matter if you have a lot of money or have achieved many professional successes? Most likely not. You'll probably reflect with sadness on all the beautiful moments that your desire for more has robbed you of.

We are constantly comparing our successes and accomplishments to those of others. It is critical to recognize that you are good, just as nature created you. Stop comparing yourself to others because there will always be someone who is further ahead, earns more money, or has a better reputation than you. But how do you know this person is happy? Presumably, the pressure of living up to one's reputation weighs heavily on those who appear to be successful.

Furthermore, when compared to another's life, this person will earn less money, have a poor reputation, and be less advanced. To be free of this constant comparison against everything around you, you must find happiness and peace of mind within yourself, independent of the recognition of others.

But how can you break the cycle of constantly comparing yourself to others? To do so, you must first understand the mechanism of comparison. People compare because they set standards for themselves. Envy, pity, and even resentment can arise due to this mechanism. How does this realization help you break free from the concept of competition? First, you should develop your standards independent of others while also appreciating, accepting, and growing from their feedback and evaluation. Be flexible in evaluating situations and actions and setting new standards for personal growth. Even defeat can provide you with insights and lessons for the future.

There are various methods for removing negative thoughts and making room for new, optimistic, and stimulating thoughts. To do so, you must first recognize your definition of happiness because happiness is always an individual experience. Naturally, not all tips and methods are suitable for you. Undoubtedly, you will come across information and possibilities that will help you develop yourself and positively direct your thoughts. It is important to maintain discipline at all times and to try out some methods for a while. You will need to invest some time in this at first. Grow gradually, start slowly, and persevere!

No one-size-fits-all solution will change your entire thought pattern with a single application. For the time being, you must establish every habit and thought pattern. Great information will motivate you to approach the subject of happiness, positive thinking, and self-discovery with motivation: simply dealing with the issue - with yourself – positively influences your feelings.

In general, a free and happy mind is always dependent on a sense of gratitude. Many studies have already proven that you will immediately feel happier when you start appreciating the little things and opening your eyes to the beauty of life. Furthermore, an open mind that approaches life with curiosity and ventures into new, uncharted territories is always happier. Begin exploring your options, recognizing your potential, and finding great paths for the future.

This chapter will teach you four methods for positively influencing your thought patterns. You will learn how to tell yourself to go through life mindfully, allowing you to appreciate the splendor and beauty of small things with the ease of a child.

Growing Through Further Training

Our mind craves information because the nature of our brain makes us eager to learn new things. New impressions, paths, and situations inspire us to expand beyond ourselves. Read, learn, and educate yourself about where you can go, how to keep your body healthy, and how to open your mind. You become more inventive and discover new ways to achieve your goals. You broaden your horizons in this way: the unthinkable becomes a reality.

Do you still struggle to direct your concentration and focus? It's no surprise in this day and age. Our attention span has decreased significantly since the invention of the internet and the ability to access information anytime. Everything is moving faster, videos are getting shorter, and sources of distractions have increased. While it's true that the internet offers us an incredible amount of opportunities, we should still get away from it regularly, especially while we're learning outside of it. Your learning environment also significantly impacts how well you absorb and process information. Positive vibrations and emotions favor this – fear, restlessness, and a negative mood, on the other hand, paralyze the absorption of new information. Sometimes, classical music in the background can help. Positive vibrations – music, for example - release dopamine, your body's happiness hormone. Your memory function and association skills increase right away. It makes sense to create circumstances that cause you to release dopamine before learning or working. To actively trigger dopamine release, dance and sing a little, eat your favorite food, or take a walk.

Free the Mind with Fresh Air

Get outside and enjoy nature! The fresh air from a walk, a picnic, or quiet moments by the sea or lake clears your mind and recharges it. At the same time, it's important to leave your gadgets at home or turn them off so you can escape the hustle and bustle of humanity. You can enjoy and take in the small things, such as a bird chirping, the sound of the water, and all the other noises and fragrances of nature. Of course, reading a book while doing this is also a pleasant companion as you unwind in tune with nature.

Mindfulness Exercises

You will quickly notice a significant difference if you know your happiness or train yourself to open your vision to it. After a short time, you will become more attentive, notice the small, beautiful things in life, and directly see an increase in your satisfaction if the gratitude comes from the heart. Although it may be challenging to experience genuine gratitude at first, after some time, it will eventually come to pass and come true. Gratitude also strengthens your positive feelings and helps you to become more aware of your previous state. Many people have already noticed this effect and have begun keeping *gratitude diaries*.

Initially, it will be difficult because the negative thinking pattern does not dissolve overnight. It requires training. Integrate a small mindfulness exercise into your daily routine. If you find the exercise difficult at first, you can do it once a week as a final reflection on the previous days. Regularity will help you cement a new way of thinking, allowing you to develop a positive attitude toward yourself and all the little things in life.

To do this, ask yourself the following questions at regular intervals in the morning and write down the answer in your diary:

- What three things are you grateful for today?

- What event could make today/the coming week a wonderful one?

- What do you like/did you like about yourself today/last week?

On the same day, in the evening, answer three more questions:

- How did you help another person today?

- What can you do better the following day/week?

- What did you like most about today/this week?

The desire to do anything grows automatically when you think positively, reflect on your life, and become oriented toward wonderful things. You sharpen your focus on the present and steadily enable yourself to take small steps. As a result, your mind expands, steers away from worries, and opens new doors for you. You learn to control your thoughts to perceive your environment more positively in the future. Learn to maintain a clear perspective and respond to stimuli in a controlled manner. Furthermore, small compliments help you in accepting yourself as a person. Constant self-criticism, on the other hand, paralyzes you and reduces your range of action: you lose trust in yourself and bind your mind.

Smile

Even a conscious smile causes your body to release hormones that influence your level of happiness. When you feel happy, your mind charges up with energy. In many cases, it has been demonstrated that heartfelt smiles follow intentional smiles. You radiate positive energy and draw people to you almost magically. A smile can relieve tension in yourself and the group dynamics, even in stressful or difficult situations with multiple people. A positive attitude toward yourself and others make life much easier. New doors open, new acquaintances are made, and you make room to discover yourself as a positive person.

Great Methods for a Strong Mind

A happy life is determined not by how your life is structured or what initial conditions exist but by the perspective you take on your life and how you interpret situations. The degree to which your mind is liberated and happy is determined by gratitude, the realization that even the most difficult strokes of fate contain a lesson, and the understanding that you are in charge of your own happiness. The strength of your sense of living a self-determined life also plays a role in this. Different things make you feel like you're in charge of your life, that you reach your full potential, and that you're happy. This includes broadening your mind emotionally, as emotional intelligence is essential for personal happiness.

Empathy enables you to express your feelings, understand your surroundings, and interpret the emotions of others, allowing you to avoid painful situations. The thought of causing harm to another person negatively impacts your mind. People who take pleasure in the suffering of others, in particular, are prone to toxic behavior and are blind to their happiness. Emotional intelligence encourages you to keep your emotional world stable and your composure in the face of setbacks so that you can reflect on your reactions and open your mind to the setback's lesson.

In addition, the following four personality traits are required for a liberated mind:

- Compatibility

- Extroversion

- Openness

- Conscientiousness

Having an outgoing personality can help if you want to stabilize and expand your social environment. Since not all introverts are necessarily unhappy, it might be challenging to change one's personality from an introvert to an extrovert. Your sense of self, self-satisfaction, and openness to new experiences are fundamental prerequisites for growth. You radiate this satisfaction. Other people will sense this and consider the time spent with you a blessing, making you feel valued and acknowledged. Introverts with a clear mind and a happy inner life can appreciate the small things in life and have a strong sense of personal happiness.

Forgiveness

When Nelson Mandela was released from prison, he said, "If I continue to hate these people, I will stay in prison." Ongoing hatred, growing anger, and the tenacity of one's rage draw bad things to one almost magically. What various religions teach is also essential for an atheist seeking happiness. Forgiveness, self-lessness, and gratitude are key elements for a positive thought structure. Buddhism has formulated a moving metaphor for this: Those who hold on to anger are symbolically holding a glowing piece of coal – the only person who gets burned is oneself. For-giveness, thus, is essential to relax a tense mind. The motto "*A person who forgives has a liberated mind*" also states that having a positive outlook on others directly increases one's well-being.

You can let go of negative emotions and tensions by forgiving others. Holding onto negative emotions like rage, disappoint-ment, and sadness makes them stay with you. By staying above things, you can allow yourself to feel better about yourself and the people around you. This will, at the very least, enable you to fully detach from negative thought patterns. After someone has harmed you, you may wonder, "Why did the person act that way? Why is this happening to me? Why did the person want to hurt me?" However, these questions only encourage a downward spiral. Instead, try to think about the bigger picture. Recognize that the actions of others reveal more about them than what it says about you. As soon as you realize that contact with certain people continuously upsets you, it would be best to consider disengaging from these toxic relationships without anger and resentment.

Meditation

While many people associate meditation with spirituality and therefore dismiss it as a method of relaxation and self-discovery, science has repeatedly confirmed that meditation – which involves consciously letting go and relaxing – significantly impacts mental health. It frees you from reliance on external sources of happiness, allowing you to determine your own satisfaction and, thus, support your mind as it unfolds. It eliminates reliance on outside happiness, allowing you to establish your own level of contentment and assist your mind's development in this way. By regularly giving your body and mind a break, your ability to concentrate and your motivation will increase. Furthermore, remaining calm in tense situations and reflectively finding a sensible solution is easier. There are many apps available that can help you with your meditation. However, if you want to be self-sufficient, here is a step-by-step guide that will allow you to benefit from these great methods:

1. Find a quiet, undisturbed place. Put away any devices or distractions that make noise and put on warm, comfortable clothes so your motionless body doesn't cool down during meditation. You can also brighten the atmosphere by lighting a few candles.

2. Get into a comfortable position. You can lie, sit, or stand - the main thing is that you feel comfortable and your body is stable to stay in the position for a while.

3. Stand, lie down, or sit with your spine straight. Allow your shoulders to relax slightly and release any tension. Slight-

ly tilt your head towards your chest, and your hands are resting on your body, either on your thighs or your belly.

4. Initially, you will probably find it difficult to let go of your thoughts and keep your mind clear. Therefore, start with shorter sessions. In the beginning, about 5 minutes is enough. Gradually increase the time over a few weeks until the meditation lasts 15 to 20 minutes. To do this, set your alarm clock to a gentle tone that will gradually bring you out of meditation after the specified time.

5. Have you started the meditation properly? Then you are finally ready to get started. You must pay attention to your breathing throughout the exercise because it relaxes and stabilizes your stressed and active mind. If you find it difficult to keep your mind on your breathing, you can concentrate on relaxing specific muscle groups. Begin by loosening the muscle groups on your head, such as your jaw, forehead, and neck. Slowly move down your body, focusing on releasing each muscle tension until you reach your feet. When you have relaxed all the muscles individually, shift your focus to the relaxation of the entire body and watch how it reacts.

6. Suppose you take a break from the hustle and bustle and give yourself a moment of peace, your stressful and burdensome thoughts will soon catch up with you. This also happens during meditation and is not a problem at all. Accept and embrace your thoughts as your own. However, it is time to let them go during the next moment. Visualize

yourself letting go of your thoughts. To do this, imagine that your thoughts are passing you by like clouds in the sky or that you are packing your belongings into a train slowly moving away from you.

7. Once your alarm clock takes you out of meditation, it's time to slowly, quietly return. You should also set aside some minutes for this. Open your eyes, take a deep breath, stretch your body, and slowly straighten up, vertebra by vertebra. Allow yourself a moment of peace and quiet, for example, with a cup of tea.

Listen to Music

Listening to relaxing music – especially singing along and dancing to it – has a meditative effect as it relieves tension and excess energy. According to research, listening to positive music releases endorphins which provide a feeling of happiness. Eating your favorite food or exercising has similar effects. Some songs even resonate with a message that enriches your life as a result of this process. Singing and dancing with others also promote the feeling of being a part of something larger, which strengthens interpersonal relationships.

Optimism

Those who believe that something good will happen to them begin to shape their destiny. Imagining positive things encourages an optimistic thought process. However, optimism should not be stifled to the point where it becomes dependent on the outcome of specific situations, as this can lead to feelings of disappointment. This also causes you to lose sight of what is truly important – the bigger picture, the beauty in the little things, and a positive, self-sufficient sense of self-worth. In contrast, a healthy, optimistic mindset leads you to integrating a pattern that will support you even in the face of setbacks and moments of sadness and will help you correctly interpret situations and feelings: as a lesson.

Writing

Many people find that writing has a favorable impact on their minds. Through writing, you may unwind, reflect, and improve yourself. As a result, writing becomes a source of new inspiration and energy for you. When you write in your diary or on a sheet of paper, you are alone with yourself – free yourself from the pressure and desire to receive recognition for your actions and words! During the writing process, you will learn to clarify your thoughts, which will help you articulate your needs precisely in future conversations. It's always a good idea to pen something positive at the end of the writing process, such as something you're grateful for. This will reinforce an optimistic thought structure.

Every person is exposed to the danger of being trapped in their own experiences and past. However, many people are not aware of this fact. They live an unreflective life, letting the chains remain and depriving themselves of the joy of life. You relax the moment you take a moment to reflect on yourself and identify your priorities. You almost automatically begin to understand your desires and feelings as you write. Find out what you need to change in your life! Writing allows you to heal and indulge yourself. This also changes how you interact with other people: you learn your limits, can express yourself, and prioritize yourself and your happiness, which makes social interaction easier.

The Not-to-Do List

The constant pressure of living up to the expectations of our work, loved ones, and friends paralyze us. We quickly forget what gives us strength and where we get new energy to meet the demands of daily life: alone time. With the *not-to-do list*, you can avoid the downward spiral of having to do more and more tasks and stressing your mind, which especially challenges the doers among us at first.

This is where you remind yourself daily which obligations you don't have to fulfill (today). With this list, you will learn to cut back and set limits by prioritizing tasks. You can only get the strength, time, and space you need for tasks and demands that make you happy if you learn to do without. Many people find it difficult to let go of something. After all, this is tantamount to a sense of loss, so your self-confidence and self-image may be distorted. This is where you remind yourself every day of which obligations you don't have to fulfill (today). With this list, you will learn to cut back and set limits by prioritizing tasks. Only by learning to do without will you gain the strength, time, and space to devote to tasks and demands that lead to your happiness. Many people find it difficult to let go of something. After all, this is a loss, and your self-confidence and self-image may be distorted. That is why this is a learning process – you must learn to prioritize and focus on important things over others to manage your power reserves carefully.

Time for Yourself

Too many tasks and material possessions strain you, so it's crucial to find the right balance between work and life so that your private life isn't affected by your professional one. Of course, your job must also provide you with this opportunity. Many employers have little sensitivity about how much of a burden their employees are under. The key here is to set boundaries and, if necessary, to reject an employer if you are overworked. Nobody wants you to collapse from exhaustion and ultimately be unable to perform your job and live your private life with a burn-out syndrome. To prevent this, make time for yourself and fill it with everything that makes you happy. You can also take a break to relax and unwind. You have complete control here. At the very least, turn off your smartphone during this so that no one disturbs you in your free time. According to recent studies, people are constantly occupied with their smartphones to be reachable. They check their phones 76 times per day. This occurs approximately every 18 minutes throughout the day, so give yourself some real time off without the pressure of having to comply with other people's wishes.

Back to Nature

Scientists have found that a daily 15-minute walk in nature boosts personal life satisfaction while also strengthening your heart and immune system. This significantly lowers the risk of having a stroke or a heart attack. What is the reason for this?

The location plays a decisive role here. Two independent research teams examined two groups in a study. One took a walk in nature, the other in the city. In the first group, the researchers noted increased lung capacity and stabilized blood pressure after the walk, while in the second group, no difference was noted from before the walk. Spending time in nature is truly rejuvenating. The pleasant sounds, the earthy smell, the oxygen-rich forest air, the escape from the restless, crowded city, and the vibrant colors are a real treat for your spirit. Here, you can escape the daily grayness of the city and reconnect with nature. Nature exudes tranquility that we cannot find anywhere else. The sound of the chirping birds and rustling leaves surrounds you to soothe your spirit.

Many people believe that a walk will never have the same effect as sweat-inducing sports, but this is incorrect. Both sports and walks have been scientifically proven to have a similar effect on your mental and physical health. For example, a person weighing 80 kilograms burns 240 calories during a 4-kilometer walk. He only burns 80 calories more if he runs that distance. This minor difference is due to the fact that walking requires significantly more steps than running, which activates your muscles.

Self-Acceptance

All of the previous findings are related to one big picture: accepting yourself as a person. The constant debate with yourself, the constant self-criticism, the internal conflict – it all paralyzes your entire personality. It is essential to think of yourself as a friend and treat yourself as you would one. Forgive yourself for your mistakes and start viewing them as learning opportunities! Practicing mindfulness, such as speaking kindly to yourself, can lead you to discover who you are. Language has a huge impact on your self-esteem. Simply saying things positively will even inspire you to try something new. It is always better to take chances than to do nothing. While the statement "No one has ever done it!" creates an immediate barrier, the phrases "Many try their hand at it!" or "You only have to try something enough times to master it!" are far more motivating.

If you constantly give yourself negative feedback, you will become stagnant. On the other hand, positive reinforcement and a positive outlook will extend your perspective, improving your quality of life as a whole. Encourage yourself, put some effort into it, and recognize your value. Everyone will experience failure when attempting to try things; this is normal and can teach us a lot so that the next attempt will undoubtedly succeed.

Learn to accept when you are exhausted and replenish your energy by going for a stroll or immersing yourself in a book. In the same way, open your eyes to your strengths and potential, then use them to your advantage so you can live a happy and fulfilling life.

Learn to Say No

Many people think openness means saying yes to everything and taking on every adventure and task to grow. Many people experience a sense of missing out because life has so much to offer. However, it is impossible to see and experience everything while still knowing who you are. Adventures are great, as is going beyond your comfort zone, but it's also important to cut back and focus on what will propel you forward.

Anyone who constantly imposes new responsibilities on himself, pushing himself beyond his limits, is doing no one any favors. None of them are in his field of interest, even if he fulfills them passionately. The urgency to complete everything by a specific time makes it impossible to learn from the task or even to take pleasure in the downtime. The result is stress, confusion, exhaustion, negativity, and insomnia. If you, too, have been unable to keep up with your tasks, now is the time to say no to those things that tend to hold you back from achieving your goals or are not a priority for you.

Only someone who can say no has the courage to pursue what truly launches him forward in life. A man affirms many things that he does not want to do. Some affirmations make sense, such as that your child should have a decent education, even if they don't feel like coming to school so that they may make thoughtful decisions later in life. However, these are exceptions, and as I'm sure you know: exceptions prove the rule.

You've probably felt powerless at some point because you've taken on too much. Frustration sets in quickly and you don't know which things to prioritize. Even activities that bring you joy can quickly become a burden when you feel pressured to do everything. At the same time, you are never compelled to constantly go beyond your own limits to help others, perform tasks, and overburden yourself. Those who lead such a lifestyle will most likely reach their mental and physical limits at some point. Many people have suffered from a burn-out syndrome, stroke, or heart attack due to being overworked. Stress affects your entirely – both inside and out. It's incredibly important to learn to relinquish tasks, not to consider every task a chore, and to simply say no. By withdrawing from situations that don't suit you and delegating tasks to others, you gain a lot of time for yourself, which is incredibly good for you. Every time you commit to something, you deny yourself the opportunity to do something else with your time. Whenever you do something that you do not enjoy, you block opportunities for yourself. As a result, a no is always a decision to shape your future time, whereas a yes is a commitment. Take some time to think about how you want to spend your time.

In the process of self-discovery, saying no is incredibly important. You don't have time for positive thoughts when you're under constant stress. Without the ability to say no to things, you will never find out what makes you truly happy. Everything that stands in the way of your success should be outright rejected. This does not mean that you should not help others move or not feed your friends' cats while they're on vacation – friendships are also crucial to your happiness. However, there is a difference between taking on everything and doing your friends a small favor. Always keep your goals in mind and stay focused. Choose where you invest your time and energy wisely!

Why is it so Hard for Us to Reject Something?

Most of the time, we take on responsibilities because we think we want to. However, this will do not stem from the depths of our personality but rather from the desire for recognition: we want other people to like us and to appear friendly or helpful. We are more likely to say yes when asked to do something by people we frequently interact with, such as friends, family, or coworkers. We want to help the people we like, which makes it difficult to say no to their requests. The fear of jeopardizing the relationship prevents us from recognizing our actual needs. Likewise, the fear that this person would no longer be there for you if you needed them could hold you back. It is important to phrase your response correctly. A no is not unkind per se. Lovingly but directly explain why you can't accommodate a request. Would you be upset if a friend told you they couldn't do something for you because they barely had time to meet their own needs? Probably not, because we should not expect anyone to sacrifice every last ounce of their strength for us. Besides, someone struggling cannot properly support you even with their best intentions in mind.

Begin listening to your body and mind to guide yourself to happiness. A bit of procrastination can often help get rid of impulsive behavior. Listen to yourself and realize how much power you have, and decide whether a task, a meeting, or whatever it may be will bring you personal happiness.

How to Say No

People usually react instinctively. If someone is nice to you, you will go out of your way to help them if they ask, even if the task doesn't seem like it would be a good fit for you or takes up valuable time that you could be spending on other activities. The British economist Tim Harford has suggested the following method to help you choose between yes and no.

Simply ask yourself: *If I had to do this task today, would I say yes to it?* By asking this question, you are setting your priorities straight. You will clearly define your priorities if your desire is strong enough to put off other tasks. Otherwise, they will most likely weigh you down. After you have made a commitment to someone, it will be much harder for you to back out than to say no in advance.

Sure, you will often forget to ask yourself if you really want to do the task. But as soon as you think about it, use this method to solidify a thought pattern that prioritizes your needs. You will gradually improve your ability to reject tasks and immediately open new doors that hold great opportunities for you over time.

If you find it difficult at first to say no to a request, you can avoid this through proper wording. For example, if your colleague asks you to cover their shift, you can decline the request without saying no – instead, you could say, "Unfortunately, I have already made a commitment that day." It's the same with new projects. Does your employer want to give you a new project, but you're already fully loaded with your current one? Communicate this by saying, "I'll finish my current project first and get back to you after." As you can see, there are ways to avoid this seemingly heavy word and still turn down a task. Take your time learning to say no. No one likes you less when you turn down their request because this is part of everyday life. Focus on the tasks that are your top priority. Of course, you can take on additional responsibilities, provided that you have the time for it.

Your Body as a Vessel for a Healthy Mind

Your body and your mind are strongly intertwined. This also appears several times in different German proverbs:

- They are one heart and soul.

- The problem hits me in the stomach.

- The pain breaks my heart.

It is clear that mental health has a significant impact on physical integrity. This connection was also highlighted in the previous chapter when the optimist and pessimist were presented. However, many studies have also proven the mind-body connection the other way around. Accordingly, for a stable mental state, it is equally important to treat your body with respect and care so that your mind feels at home in it – otherwise, they will be in conflict with each other. Several factors play a crucial role here and this chapter will teach you how to directly strengthen your mind by observing them in your daily life.

Balanced Sleep: Recharge Your Energy Reserves

Your entire mental and physical health depends on whether you get enough sleep. It is not without reason that there is a large body of literature devoted solely to this topic in the context of physical and mental illnesses. Insomnia affects up to 90% of all people at some point in their lives, and the number is growing. This is partly due to society's increasing demands for performance and activity, which strongly emphasize mental and physical health as key qualities for both professional and personal success. Phrases like "You can sleep when you're dead!" or "Nothing comes from sleeping!" demonstrate that negative societal reactions can still follow balanced sleep behavior. For instance, the *microsleep* phenomenon is occurring more frequently due to general exhaustion in society. Performance, responsiveness, and overall health are closely linked to your sleep behavior.

Our society's emphasis on performance can put us under constant stress, which can negatively affect how we sleep. Examples of insufficient or restless sleep triggers include professional pressure, mental stress, physical pain (such as from prolonged computer use), and restless thinking. Additionally, permanent accessibility, which has crept into our daily lives since the invention of the first mobile phone, poses a major problem for our recovery phases. This has less to do with work making our lives more difficult and more to do with poor time management. Many people are finding it increasingly difficult to truly unplug. As a result of social needs and permanent accessibility, many people use their smartphones and lie in their beds scrolling through social media or checking their most recent work emails before going to bed, which can sometimes have a negative impact on their thoughts. They expose themselves to blue light, which also causes sleep disruption. A permanently disturbed sleep rhythm initially affects your stress level. This increases the risk of infectious diseases because the lack of sleep weakens your immune system. The increased stress level can even be followed by heart disease.

Fortunately, our body warns us when it needs rest. However, it is important to keep an eye out for these warning signals. You will initially feel tired, exhausted, and slightly stressed. These feelings indicate the first signs of sleep deprivation. Do you remember similar feelings when your body needed rest? How did you react?

In today's society, most people react to the first signs of exhaustion with caffeinated drinks or stimulants. They fight against their own body. As a result, their body develops a chronic condition accompanied by fatigue and elevated stress levels, which causes their quality of life to suffer.

The longer you ignore your body's warning signs and continue to engage in poor sleeping habits, the worse the consequences will be. The symptoms will slowly creep in: you feel listless, easily irritated, find it difficult to concentrate on your tasks, and experience a slight tingling sensation throughout your body. With less than 4 hours of sleep per night and more than 14 hours of waking time, you are more likely to have attention problems and performance deficits. This is especially dangerous while driving a car, where unexpected risky situations can arise, leaving you unable to react properly and injuring yourself or others in the worst-case scenario.

You will feel slightly intoxicated if you continue to deprive your body of sleep. After about 18 hours, the deficits are comparable to a 0.5 alcohol level. You feel euphoric because your stressed body is trying to keep you alive by releasing dopamine in your brain, a chemical that makes you feel good. You feel amped up and intoxicated, and further withdrawal can cause you to hallucinate. Now comes a troubling realization – sleep deprivation is a direct result of stress and lack of sleep. This downward spiral must be broken as soon as the first signs appear.

Fortunately, there are methods that can help you with your sleep pattern to give your body the rest it desires. These methods will be presented to you in more detail below. On the other hand, working with your mind and physical activity have a direct positive effect on your sleep. When you exercise, you can burn off excess energy that prevents you from falling asleep at night. Similarly, a relaxed and balanced mind encourages you to let go of your thoughts before falling asleep.

Analyze Your Sleep Behavior Using A Sleep Diary

To tailor the methods to your specific needs, you must first determine how much sleep your body requires and identify any other causes of sleep problems. The German Society for Sleep Research and Sleep

Medicine recommends using a sleep diary, a proven method used in sleep research for tracking down sleep disorders and problems.

Here you document all important aspects of your sleep behavior that could be related to sleep problems, for example, the time you go to bed, the time you wake up, or even the intake of medication or alcohol. You can easily keep this log on your own, without the help of a second person, and get great insights about yourself.

In most cases, keeping a sleep diary for about two weeks is advisable. However, this is the bare minimum; a shortened log over a shorter period is not recommended. To ensure that you keep the diary regularly, keep it near your bed.

You can find a template for the sleep diary on the Internet. Simply type "Sleep Quality Questionnaire (PSQI)" into your search engine to get started. In this context, PSQI stands for the Pittsburgh Sleep Quality Index – a questionnaire designed to help you identify the severity of your sleep disorders.

If you decide to use a classic diary, then you should answer the following questions here every morning:

- At what time did you go to bed?

- What time did you fall asleep?

- Did you wake up during the night? If so, how often and at what times?

- How long did you lie awake in bed at night (including before falling asleep and after waking up)?

- What time did you wake up in the morning?

- Did you consume alcohol or medication before going to bed? If yes, what and how much?

- What was your mood on the last evening?

- How tired did you feel last evening?

- How tired do you feel this morning?

- What is your mood this morning?

After the said two weeks, start evaluating your diary. Take a calculator and start by calculating the average values of the first and second week separately. Of course, you only have to consider those questions you have answered with a number. You calculate the mean values by adding up the total numbers of an aspect and dividing by the number of those you have considered. A sleep duration of less than 6.5 hours may be an indication of a sleep disorder. However, this varies from person to person because people's need for sleep varies greatly.

The next step is to calculate your sleep efficiency. This is the ratio of how much time you spend in bed to how much time you actually sleep. In this case, a percentage value of 50 indicates that you were awake for half of the time you were in bed. The time spent in bed is determined by the time you went to bed and the time you got up the following day. Evening reading in bed is, therefore, part of the bedtime. To determine sleep efficiency, use the rule of three. If the total bedtime is 8 hours and you spent 3 of them awake in bed, the total is 8 and is 100%. To find out what percent an hour is in this context, divide 100 by 8 and get a value of 12.5, which you multiply by the time you lay awake in bed, which is 3. As a result, you have a value of 37.5%, which says that you spent more than one-third of the time lying in bed awake. Sleep efficiency is the time you actually slept, which is 62.%. However, this value is extremely critical. As a rule, sleep efficiency should have a value of 85% to 90%. As you get older, the limit drops to 80 percent. However, keep in mind that healthy sleep efficiency does not always correlate with good sleep quality.

Lastly, consider how frequently you wake up. As you get older, this value increases. Generally, waking up one to three times per night is not a cause for concern. If this value rises and you have an increased waking frequency, it could be an indication of a sleep disorder. A consultation with your doctor may help determine the cause.

Also, always look at your mood and how tired you feel throughout the day. If you feel particularly fit on any given day, mark your sleep duration to see how much sleep your body actually needs. Both too much and too little sleep can negatively affect your mind and body.

The Epworth Sleepiness Scale: Identify Your Tendency to Fall Asleep

If you also feel sluggish and sleepy throughout the day despite improved sleep patterns, you can take it a step further with the *Epworth Sleepiness Scale*. With the help of a questionnaire, you determine whether you have an increased tendency to fall asleep. In this context, values above 10 indicate a strong tendency to fall asleep during the day. If you manage to obtain this value despite trying all of the suggested methods and still see no change, you should consult your doctor. A blood test may be able to help identify a vitamin or nutrient deficiency.

Methods for Sleep Hygiene

Sleep hygiene deals with different behavior and conditions that help promote healthy sleep. You can improve your sleep behavior by using various sleep hygiene methods. However, the term *"hygiene"* is used differently in this context than what you are familiar with. It is primarily about learning different methods for calming yourself down and falling asleep faster. The different methods are briefly and clearly summarized here for you:

- You should only use your own bed for sleeping as much as possible. Eating, drinking coffee in the morning, and reading a book should all take place on the sofa or elsewhere. In this way, you condition your body to rest in bed and you will find it much easier to fall asleep after a certain period of time.

- Cut your bedtime down to when you actually sleep. Many people spend a significant amount of time dozing in bed, either in the morning or earlier in the evening. This helps lower your sleep pressure during the deep sleep phase. That is why you should get up when you are no longer really asleep, especially in the morning.

- Avoid taking a nap, especially if you are working on your sleep rhythm and can't rest at night. Otherwise, you may not be tired enough to fall asleep in the evening.

- Avoid potential sources of distraction in your bedroom, such as the television, the telephone, and, if possible, your smartphone. An analog alarm clock is more than enough to wake you up.

- Make sure your bedroom is properly ventilated before going to bed, as fresh air promotes healthy sleep patterns.

- Enough exercise throughout the day can release excess energy in your body that keeps you from falling asleep. However, you should avoid doing sports right before going to bed because they stimulate your circulation, which also stimulates your mind.

- If possible, avoid eating anything 2 to 3 hours before going to bed. This stimulates circulation and can make it difficult to fall asleep.

- You should also avoid drinking alcoholic beverages 5 hours before sleeping to give your body enough time to break them down.

- If stress and recurring thoughts keep you awake at night, a diary can be a true friend in difficult times. You can use the diary to let go of negative feelings and stressful thoughts while also experiencing positive feelings throughout your sleep and beyond.

- Our sleep rhythm has become increasingly disrupted since the invention of artificial light. In the past, fatigue came automatically with darkness. We can now find our way around thanks to the lamps inside and outside the house. As a result, our sleep rhythm suffers. If you have trouble falling asleep, avoid bright light for 2 hours before bedtime and replace it with a cozy little lamp or candles.

- Nature also provides us with true miracle remedies in the context of our own sleeping behavior. Lavender oil has been proven to have a positive effect not only on your sleep but also on your psyche. According to studies, it contains ingredients that have a calming and sleep-inducing effect.

- Lastly, bedtime rituals are a great way to get your body ready for sleep. You can induce sleep and help your mind wind down by listening to relaxing music, practicing muscle relaxation reflexes, or simply listening to sounds of nature.

The Effects of A Healthy Diet: "You Are What You Eat"

In many cases, the adage "You are what you eat!" may prove to be true again and again because your eating habits directly influence not only your body but also your entire mood, being, and mind. Many studies have also come to this conclusion. Essential minerals and vitamins that influence your mental health are obtained through your diet – when you lack important nutrients, you feel tired, weak, and unmotivated to cope with daily life. In addition, a healthy diet also affects your physical appearance. Despite the fact that this is problematic, when we socialize, our bodies are frequently exposed to several forms of objective evaluation. In the best-case scenario, we break away from these ideals and learn to love and accept ourselves as nature created us. Although it can be challenging to completely let go of these thought patterns, physical activity and change directly impact your self-image. You feel beautiful because any positive change, no matter how small, feels good. It's important to establish the right goals to achieve this. Throughout the book, you will find valuable information which will help you with your self-improvement in the best possible way.

Your gut is another factor linked to mental health and a healthy diet. The gut-brain axis is a network of nerve cells connecting your gut to your brain. In this case, the hormone *serotonin* is essential for your mental stability. Your intestines produce 95%of this hormone, which keeps your mind consistently positive. An unhealthy gut can cause serotonin deficiency and even promote mental illness because inflammatory signals in your gut can travel to your brain and trigger negative moods.

Nerve cells, immune messengers, intestinal hormones, and bacteria thus have an influence on your emotions. This was also investigated in a study from Australia with 3,000 test subjects where those who ate healthy, nutrient-rich foods showed improved mental health over time than those who ate high-fat, high-sugar diets. Additionally, you can support your gut by eating probiotic yogurt with numerous strains of the same bacteria. Dietary fiber, which can be obtained from whole grain products, is also a key component of healthy digestion. These are some of the best ways to keep your intestinal flora healthy.

A Mediterranean diet can help reduce inflammation levels in the intestines when experiencing acute intestinal problems. The diet includes fresh vegetables, olive oil, fish, nuts, whole grains, or similar products rich in Omega-3 fatty acids.

However, changing your entire diet overnight is not easy: your upbringing, habits, and discipline all influence how easily you can integrate a new diet into your life. Several approaches can help you achieve your goals based on your mental and physical capabilities, which you will learn more about later. First, you'll discover which foods are essential for a healthy diet.

What Does a Balanced Diet Look Like?

You need a healthy intake of vitamins and nutrients so that your body has enough energy to complete all your tasks while also having enough energy left over to engage in fulfilling activities and keep your mind happy. The food pyramid provides some guidelines for this, as shown below:

- Try to drink at least 1.5 liters of water daily so your body can flush out germs, among other things.

- It is also recommended to consume three servings of vegetables per day, such as one bell pepper, one carrot, and one onion.

- In addition, your body requires enough carbohydrates to absorb fiber. Experts recommend three servings per day in this case as well.

- A variety of fruits, nuts, and legumes contain numerous vitamins that help to strengthen your immune system. Nutritionists recommend two servings of fruit or a handful of legumes or nuts to meet your nutritional needs.

- Your body also needs Omega-3 fatty acids to remain physically and mentally stable. Therefore, try to eat fatty fish or low-fat meat products two to three times a week. If you follow a vegan diet, there are great alternatives to meet your Omega-3 fatty acid needs.

- Keep your fat and sugar intake as low as possible. The German Federal Center for Nutrition recommends consuming a maximum of two portions of fats and oils a day. In this case, vegetable fats clearly outperform animal fats. Other foods high in fat, sugar, or salt destabilize mental and physical health. According to the Federal Center for Nutrition, you should eat no more than one portion of these a day.

How Sport Enriches Your Life

Little to no exercise can have serious consequences not only for your body but also for your mind. Aside from obesity, shortened ligaments, muscle tension, or cardiac arrhythmias, low body utilization causes a stressed mind and, in the worst case, depressive moods. The energy you consume through food must be used in some way. If unused, this energy will be stored in your body as fat deposits. A large number of fat storage, insulin resistance, and, in some cases, high blood pressure amplifies stress. Small problems can quickly pull the rug out from under you. Your body and mind should always be your top priority if you want to live a beautiful and happy life. Even a short walk can reduce the risk of mental and physical illness.

Exercise is a real natural remedy that is extremely beneficial to both your soul and body in every way. It expels excess energy, boosts stress resistance, clears the mind of negative thoughts, and creates pure freedom. During and after exercise, your body rewards you with dopamine and serotonin, the body's happiness hormones that consistently positively affect your thoughts. Specific movements have been shown to alleviate negative moods in people suffering from depression. Rhythmic movements, such as dancing, running, or skipping, are also incredibly beneficial to your mental health. According to studies, sport has a more substantial effect on the minds of people with symptoms of depression than on those with a relatively healthy psyche because the potential for improvement is higher. Furthermore, it has been shown that these rhythmic movements can sometimes work better than an antidepressant.

You also strengthen your cognitive abilities (memory function, attention, and information processing time) by getting enough exercise. You become more creative in your problem-solving approach, are less easily overwhelmed by problems, and are more focused and efficient in doing your tasks which saves you a lot of time that can be spent on physical activities or activities you enjoy.

Exercising also leads to cognitive improvements and reduces the risk of developing dementia. As a result, the benefits of exercise on the overall mind should not be overlooked. Rhythmic endurance exercise has the most significant impact on your mind (especially in the great outdoors). Any physical activity, such as weight training or walking, will help you release energy and organize your thoughts to see yourself in a better light since exercise has a meditative effect.

You can learn to love yourself and improve your life with enough initiative – you can enhance your motor skills, lessen physical discomfort that causes negativity, and link your mind and body as one. The fact that your outward appearance changes is secondary because your perception of your own body automatically changes when you move around regularly.

It is important to integrate physical exercise into your daily routine and gradually make it an unconscious habit. The fitter you become and the longer you exercise, the better your self-confidence will effectively counteract your fears during private or personal gatherings. Regular exercise will help you achieve your goals apart from learning to accept and believe in yourself.

In summary, you simply feel better if you are physically active. You can embark on more enjoyable adventures, such as hiking, without being plagued by self-doubt and fear of failure.

Improve Your Life Today: 10 Inspiring Routines

A healthy sleep pattern, a balanced diet, daily exercise, and enough personal time have all been shown to contribute to a happy life and a healthy mind and body. However, putting all of this into action is anything but simple – finding time to restructure your routine in addition to daily stress and internalized thought patterns and behaviors can be difficult for some people.

In the following chapters, you will learn how to change your habits. Large amounts of information can be overwhelming at first, but small incentives will serve as your motivation for integrating new habits and personal goals to help you gradually improve your life. The following behavioral changes, according to researchers, can have a positive impact on your mind and body. Choose when and what to incorporate at a time, and then use the valuable information in the following chapters to make long-term positive changes in your habits.

Get Up Early

Getting up early is beneficial because it is ingrained in our biorhythms to leave the bed when the sun rises. According to one study, getting up earlier reduces your risk of developing depression by 12 to 27%. This is due to your natural *day-wake rhythm*, which has been established in the human body for thousands of years.

Furthermore, the extra time you gain is a real stress reliever. All of the daily tasks that you have to manage can be spread out over a longer period while still finding time to pursue your interests.

Skip Your Morning Coffee

Many people find it hard to get out of bed in the morning, so they turn on the coffee pot right after getting up. Their day doesn't start until they have their first cup of coffee – the caffeine in the hot drink gets your blood flowing, gets rid of tiredness, and makes it easier to focus, which is why almost everyone starts their day with it. Caffeine doesn't kick in until 30 to 45 minutes after you drink it. This is how long it takes for the alkaloid to get into your bloodstream. That sounds good, right? Why should you still skip your coffee in the morning and drink it later?

After you wake up, your body releases the hormone *cortisol* at its highest peak. The stress hormone is made in your adrenal cortex. It raises your blood pressure, speeds up your metabolism, and affects your carbohydrate levels. It ensures you are awake and alert in the morning – your body makes sure you are happy when you wake up. If you drink coffee on top of that, you might feel more stressed and restless. Your body reacts instinctively as it starts to reduce the production of your body's own wake-up agent. You make yourself dependent on caffeine because your body learns that it can't get going without it.

Scientists recommend not drinking your first coffee until at least an hour after you wake up to benefit from your cortisol. Cortisol levels increase again during the day, between 12 and 1 p.m. and around 5:30 p.m. Here, however, drinking the caffeine drink is less of a problem. In general, drinking coffee in a healthy way is usually harmless. The German Federal Ministry of Food and Agriculture says this means no more than 3-4 cups of coffee daily.

Minerals, phytonutrients, and antioxidants in sugar-free coffee can even lower the risk of type 2 diabetes.

Start Your Day with A Glass of Water

Replace your morning coffee with a large glass of water. This valuable liquid stimulates your metabolism, is a core element of your blood, regulates your body temperature, and ensures the healthy transport of nutrients. However, your body can't keep this water permanently – it loses water when you sweat, loses water when you breathe, and loses water when you excrete to flush out germs. Hence, regular water intake is essential for a healthy mind and body. The German Nutrition Society recommends drinking about 1.5 liters of water a day. As soon as temperatures rise or you engage in intensive sports, you should increase your water intake accordingly.

Your body can lose up to 2 liters of water while you sleep. So, instead of your usual cup of coffee in the morning, a glass of water is a much better way to start the day. Start right away by replenishing your water supply. Drinking water on an empty stomach will stimulate your metabolism and digestion – you will also help your body get rid of the toxins that were broken down while you were sleeping.

The Breakfast Routine

Some can barely get going without a proper breakfast, while others have trouble eating anything at all. But what is the healthier alternative?

Unless you can't eat in the morning, listen to what your body tells you. The night fast will last longer if you wait until breakfast or (early) lunch. This is similar to what you may already know as *"intermittent fasting,"* a way of eating where you can only eat for about 8 to 10 hours. This makes the time between dinner and breakfast the next day 14 to 16 hours. This type of fasting lowers your blood sugar and makes your body burn more fat. As a result, it can help you lose weight, lower your risk of developing diabetes, and reduce inflammation in your body. It has a direct positive effect on your health.

If you are one of those people who needs breakfast to get through the day, it should be as healthy as possible. Support your muscles and joints by eating food rich in protein and fiber.

The Positive Effects of Morning Meditation

Mediation is an ancient, proven method that harmonizes the mind and body, sharpens your senses, and relaxes. Thus, you effectively counteract stress, pressure, and anxiety. If you start your day with meditation, it will positively affect your entire day. You can cope more, have a better mood, have a positive effect on those around you, and feel good at the end of the day.

The more often you do this, the more peace and relaxation will come into your body. Even mindfulness exercises have been tested out by scientists. Psychologists and neuroscientists found a positive effect on the brain regions that deal with stress, memory, and self-awareness. After just 8 weeks, test subjects were able to handle stress and fears better.

Do 10 Minutes of Exercise Before or After Work

Any kind of exercise is good for your body and mind, whether it's yoga, running, or lifting weights. The surprising fact is that, depending on your body type, as little as 10 to 15 minutes of exercise a day can be enough to improve your health. After the first few months, the risk of cardiovascular disease and premature death is already reduced by 14%. It's even possible to extend your life by up to 3 years through this simple routine. It's important to keep your blood pressure up for short periods of time, like when you do interval training. Be sure to continue moving your body for a short time afterwards to keep your circulation stable.

Slowly making sports a part of your daily routine is a good idea, especially for people who have never done sports before and want to get their minds used to it. Once your body gets used to exercising, you should slowly do more of it to keep getting better.

Move Every Hour for Two to Three Minutes

People who work in an office and sit a lot will notice sooner or later that the lack of movement is bad for them. In the first instance, you will see the adverse effects through back problems, slipped discs, or other physical pain. At first, the harmful effects will appear in the form of back pain, slipped discs, or other physical pain. In addition, when you sit for a long time, your metabolism slows down, and you burn fewer calories. This makes you more likely to be overweight or develop diabetes. The chance that your coronary arteries will harden and you will have a heart attack is also increased.

Most of the time, exercise alone isn't enough because the problem is that people sit for long periods of time. If you don't move for 6 to 8 hours, your body will suffer a lot. Scientists recommend moving around for a few minutes every hour. For example, you could take a short walk to a colleague's office or stretch for a bit. Set an alarm clock to go off every hour, at most.

Enjoy Some Fresh Air Every Day

Even if you don't have much time, you can always take a short 10 to 15-minute walk. Not only is it good for your body, but it also relaxes your mind and boosts your creativity. This also directly reduces the risk of cardiovascular disease and prevents depression. A short walk, ideally in nature, is already enough. If you don't have time to do this every day, you can always consider walking to work, to the grocery store, or to your friends' so that you never miss out on your daily stroll.

Put Your Smartphone Away An Hour Before Going to Bed

The constant flood of information and the way the smartphone meets our needs make us downright addicted and dependent on it. Even if it's hard, you should try to keep the important things in mind at night, which is hard to do when you're on your phone. You are also making yourself more tired because the blue light from your phone screen stops your body from producing melatonin, the hormone responsible for making you sleepy. Give your body and mind a chance to fall asleep quickly and be ready for the next day by putting away your cell phone about an hour before bedtime.

Reflect on Your Day

Keeping a diary is probably the best thing you can do to help you grow steadily, improve your memory, and get rid of negative thoughts. Write down your current thoughts and what you did at the end of each day. It doesn't matter how good or bad your writing is because this is all about you and nobody will ever be able to read what you write without your permission. You can write how your day went and what's on your mind in bullet points. You can also write down beautiful quotes you came across during the day, or your hopes and dreams. There's room for everything you care about – think of your diary as your closest friend, to whom you can tell everything without fear of being judged. This will give your mind room to be open to new experiences with passion.

Discipline as a Basic Requirement for a Successful Life

Whoever wants to find happiness must be in a constant state of change. He is constantly growing and never stops developing, which broadens the scope of his ideas and actions. Your happiness is closely linked to change. If you perform an action successfully once, you feel happy. This joy, however, quickly fades after the thirtieth time you do the same action. As you know firsthand, being in a good mood enhances your ability to learn and retain information. Are you looking for new ways to expand your horizon? You need to get out of your comfort zone if you want to have new and amazing experiences. Start by doing something new every day and integrate them into your daily routine, whether it's a workout, a new meal, or some reading. We can often find happiness and the motivation to make further changes by making even the smallest changes. The biggest obstacle is the fear of failure, which can prevent us from trying a new habit at all if we are even slightly unsure of success. The key is to overcome this mentality and learn from failure, to try things out for yourself, and to never stop doing it. Inevitably, you will experience significant changes: In time, you will get over your fear and start actively seeking out more changes after realizing how change can be good for you.

Our society is also demanding a process of change and growth. Just think of how many tasks will be taken over by artificial intelligence in the future. Further training is therefore indispensable to continue and be prepared for the world of work. After all, digitization opens up more areas of work than it actually eliminates. Constant learning is not just a basic prerequisite for the working world, but also for private life. Motivated and disciplined people benefit because they open up opportunities for self-fulfillment.

Core Information about the Habits of Man

How successfully you move through your life depends on your good and bad habits. But what are habits exactly, and why do we integrate them into our daily lives? Habits are part of our lives, both the good and the bad. It's not easy to get rid of them or replace a bad habit with a good one, especially if you don't understand how they work and how you can control yourself.

We don't even realize how much our good and bad habits shape our daily lives. These are behaviors that you perform almost automatically in a regular rhythm. Habits make life easier and you don't have to think about them as much. People no longer have to think and weigh up different options, which greatly reduces the load on your brain. They are indispensable for daily functioning. Imagine how much energy you would need if you had to think about each step while eating breakfast. Thus, habits are another thing that always saves us energy. Your brain stores processes, rewards like the feeling of being full, and essential resources for tasks that need more attention. In conclusion, habits provide stability and security, even those that are perceived as bad. This will make your daily life easier to handle and keep you from getting exhausted.

Changing a routine can take a little more time depending on the habit pattern and the person. According to scientists, this takes between 18 and 254 days. The frequency with which the desired action is performed also plays an important role here; the more often it is performed in a variety of contexts, the more quickly it will automatically become a habitual part of your routine. The various contexts play a crucial role because this is how you associate a situation with a desired behavior.

Why is it so Hard to Change Habits?

Our habits always tempt us because we save precious time and energy that we can use for other tasks. Therefore, changes will always pose a sense of danger because they require the use of resources saved up. This motivation to accomplish change does not directly go hand in hand with a change in behavior. Before you can do that, you first need to understand how habit formation works, which will help you learn how to acquire new patterns. When we want to change a habit, it's usually the classic bad behavior patterns: watching too much TV, spending too much time using smartphones, eating poorly, or the like. However, we find it particularly difficult to break bad habits because they usually reward us directly, causing the brain to make connections automatically. Once smokers consume nicotine, they start to feel relaxed again. Of course, smoking is unhealthy but the body has not yet formed any associations here. Those who stop smoking only feel positive effects after a few weeks, such as more stamina, a better complexion, and a longer life expectancy. However, the body does not link these positive effects directly to nicotine withdrawal. It is therefore important to remember that one way to do this is to reward yourself or write down your goals and when you achieve them.

You will likely encounter emotional barriers, such as fear or inner resistance, as soon as you initiate a radical change in your habits. These evoke the environmental and emotional triggers. This is especially problematic and difficult if you are aiming for a big change with a big reward. However, there are great methods you can use to finally get rid of old patterns. How does it work? You will learn on the next pages.

The Course of Classic Habit Patterns

In order to break bad habits or replace them with better ones, it is necessary to take the first step and make them visible. Begin by identifying what causes undesirable behavior. Conditioning based on a stimulus-response scheme enables the development of both positive and negative behaviors. As an example, consider eating candy. There are a few treats in your desk drawer, ready to satisfy a slight craving. At first, you reach for a candy bar because you feel a pang of hunger. Eventually, however, an automatism creeps in. As soon as you open the drawer, you automatically reach for the sweets even if you are looking for something else. You have conditioned yourself in this regard because eating sugar immediately rewards you with positive feelings. Your brain stores this automatism, so any habits run unconsciously over time. This also presents a big hurdle. Uncovering unconscious habits is never easy, but it is always the first step in sustainable change.

Behind almost every bad and good habit is a fairly simple formula. It consists of three core elements:

1. The trigger:

   What feeling, time of day or season, and place trigger a bad (or even good) habit?

2. The routine/the action:

   The routine consists of the habit itself: What activity do you engage in?

3. Reward:

   What need does the habit satisfy?

In particular, an unhealthy diet and smoking are some of the most problematic habits people have. When you eat sweets, the hormones dopamine and serotonin that make you happy are released, which makes you feel good. People who are stressed or unhappy often have unhealthy habits like eating or smoking too much. When stress comes up, the body automatically goes for something it already knows will make it feel better. This creates a link between stress and bad habits like overeating or smoking. However, there is a way to break bad habits – knowing how it works will help you stop doing it or start integrating a good habit. Once you know the trigger, you can eliminate it and find another way to meet your need.

How to Spot Bad Habits

If you want to improve your life and integrate a positive mindset in the process, you need to reflect on yourself. Observe yourself doing everything you do for a week. It is incredibly important to observe your daily routine in order to identify a bad habit. In the same way, you need to question your inner feelings, that is, the trigger for the habit and the reward after you have followed it. At best, write down your findings. This will ensure that you are aware of this mechanism. The following questions will help you recognize structures and identify bad habits:

- How does your daily routine work?

- When do you get up?

- What and when do you eat breakfast?

- What beverages do you consume daily, and how much of them do you drink?

- How do you move around?

- In what situations are you prone to negative thoughts or the desire to indulge in a bad habit? What is the trigger for the habit (for example, reaching for the smartphone when boredom sets in)?

- How do you feel when you have complied with the habit, or with what moods does your body and mind reward you? What need does the habit satisfy?

- What activities do you perform and in what time frame each day?

- When do you go to bed and how much do you sleep?

- Do you consume caffeine, nicotine, or alcohol? If yes, to what extent?

- How do you react to stressful situations?

Even small insights in everyday life serve to leave bad habits behind and integrate good ones. The moment a bad habit starts to form, i.e. when the situation that makes a behavior happen (the "*trigger*"), it helps to react directly and reflect on it. Do you reach for your cell phone as soon as you turn out the light to go to bed? Then you've already identified the trigger. What are you going to do with your phone now? Do you look for information on the web or on social media? This component represents the habit. Now, question why you are engaging in this activity. Is it because of a social need, or do you have a desire to have all knowledge? What is the reward? By definition, bad habits are no longer habits because they are always unconscious patterns of behavior.

Once you become aware of them, the habit becomes a conscious behavior, making it much easier for you to replace them with good ones. Also, try to get rid of things that set you off. When the lights go out, do you always reach for your phone? Don't even turn it on; that may help you counteract the need.

Helpful Methods to Integrate New Habits

The happiest people who have truly found themselves are in a constant process of change. Especially in today's time when so many tools make your life suddenly easier, you don't have to think for yourself very often. As a result, change is also harder – it requires methods, motivation, and a systematic approach that also requires you to take initiative. The simplicity of everyday things makes it increasingly difficult for us to take hold of them. Nevertheless, it is almost frighteningly easy to integrate new behavior patterns into everyday life with recourse to valuable information. You know how important it is to give yourself credit and find new things to do. Positive encouragement is also a great way to keep yourself going when you want to integrate a new, good habit.

Focus on your goal and imagine where you can be when you have successfully implemented this habit for a certain period of time. Never lose sight of your goal. At best, even write this down and put it somewhere you'll see every day. Realizing that you are in charge of your own life and can make changes can also help you form a new habit. Always remember how privileged you are to be able to make your own decisions. Every time you do something to shape your own life, you will feel good about it. There are many ways to help you stay disciplined and on track when forming new habits. Find out which method offers you the most value and use it to break free from your old, unreflective self and create a new, motivated version of you.

Small Steps

In the beginning, the hurdle you must overcome to integrate a new habit seems quite high. However, this is your comfortable self inhibiting you from self-development. It's never about making a complete personality change overnight, instead, it's about small stages that you gradually master on the way to your goal. When integrating a new habit, it can already help to start with just ten minutes of the activity you want to do. It is always better to pursue a new habit briefly than to stay idle. If you get too absorbed in the activity and are literally in a frenzy, you can keep doing it for as long as you like. However, if you give the process less time at the start, it will be easier for you to try new things in the future.

Pictorial Ideas

Many people are becoming less and less sure of themselves. They compare themselves to others and primarily focus on their own weaknesses. This is a major problem that brings people to a stand-still. In contrast, the courage to try something new can give you a huge boost. Start encouraging yourself and be brave enough to try new things, and you will notice how your horizons expand almost automatically. You are more likely to stick with new habits if you can imagine a positive event or situation. Thus, imagining positive moments even increases the likelihood that something good will happen to you because you are open to the world.

Get Out of Your Familiar Environments

If you stay in the same place for too long, the ceiling will fall on your head, as the saying goes. A feeling of listlessness and boredom gradually sets in: a gigantic risk that even triggers a developing depressive mood in some people. Walks, small adventures, and anything else that gets you out of your normal environment work well to change this because it's much harder to change your habits when you're in the same place you always are. This is the best way to directly adapt to a change, like if you are moving or getting a new job. In fact, this has been proven by science.

A short trip or vacation is also good for your spirit because it gives you time to reflect on your life and the chance and motivation to make significant changes when you return. Many people say that after a vacation, many people say that they feel like tackling and experiencing something new because they have obviously experienced how alive they felt due to the change. On a trip, you have the chance to take new (small) risks, meet different people and places, and thereby come to insightful realizations about your own life. Once you are out of your usual environment, the triggers of bad habits are often no longer there either. This makes it easier for you to try out new patterns of behavior and make them stick. As a result, it's easier for you to continue this behavior even after you return home.

You expand your horizons by venturing into new areas and testing your limits. Every time that you try something new, you also learn something new about yourself. You will recognize which activities make you feel good and you will become a happy, free person by constantly reflecting on yourself.

Design Your Environment

As mentioned in the previous practice tip, your environment impacts your behaviors. If you sit in the same, unchanged, and familiar four walls, you are exposed to all the stimuli that trigger your bad habits. That's why it's helpful to eliminate these external stimulus triggers if possible. For example, do you have a drawer where your sweets are? Then make sure that the drawer is cleaned out. Do you want to exercise more often? In that case, it's helpful to already pack your gym bag and put it in an obvious place in the entryway. Make sure that the environmental stimuli evoke positive behaviors. At best, you should implement this at work and in your own four walls at home.

Combine Your Activities

New habits will challenge you. You will have to keep motivating yourself in the beginning. However, there is a simple way to keep your inner hurdles as low as possible. To do this, combine the new habit you want to form with something that gives you pleasure – by doing this, you'll feel less like you "have to" do something and more like you "want to" do what you're doing. So while exercising, you can use the time to listen to your favorite music or podcast.

Tell Your Friends about Your Progress

Even if you recognize that you have already accomplished a lot, you should not underestimate your need to communicate and your desire for recognition. In our entire socialization process, recognition plays an essential role in our personality development. It shows us what behavior elicits positive and negative reactions in society, thus providing us with a guide for our identity formation. It is true that self-recognition and self-acceptance play the most significant role in the entire self-discovery process; in this way, your happiness remains as independent from external factors as possible. Nevertheless, a study conducted by the Association of Science and Technology proves that communicating your goals increases the likelihood of achieving them by 65%. If you carry out a regular ritual, like discussing your goals and progress with a friend on a weekly basis, this probability increases by as much as 95%. This adds a little bit of pressure, but it can be very helpful in the right situations.

There is an immense increase in productivity because communicating with others fosters a sense of commitment that helps you achieve your goals. Most people struggle with *cognitive dissonance* or when they strive for their own behavior to be consistent with their personal beliefs.

Furthermore, sharing your successes leads to you receiving positive encouragement. The praise and recognition of close acquaintances help you reinforce positive thought patterns and encourage you to continue following through with the habit change. So, when you set your sights on the next habit change, communicate this with a friend. Together, share and celebrate your progress, as well as setbacks, so that you increase the chance of breaking unwanted habits and integrating desired ones.

Establish New Habits

Bad habits paralyze you, thereby keeping you trapped in structures that promote negative thinking patterns. Stress levels rise when there is increased television consumption, a poor sleep rhythm, lack of exercise, or the habit of agreeing to everything, thus burdening yourself with too much. You keep your mind locked up, full of negative energy, and give yourself little space for self-development. Of course, you can never live a life where you are never stressed again, but a balanced person can deal with the cause of stress in a much more calm and reflective way and no longer see it as a reason to do something bad. Consequently, you efficiently eliminate the problem or find a way to deal with it. Also, reflecting on the positive things in life and realizing how small the problem is compared to the beauty of life will help you put yourself back in a positive mood.

Move away from the thought of changing your entire life and way of thinking from one day to the next. Give yourself space and time, and take a calm approach toward self-improvement. Just changing one thing can make a big difference in how happy you are with your life. For example, the time you save by watching half as much TV could be better spent on a new habit. Simply set a timer for yourself or decide to watch a maximum of one movie in the evening after you have done everything you set out to do for that day.

But what exactly defines a bad habit? How can you tell that an activity is not good for you? In addition to simple and understandable factors such as diet and exercise, which were discussed in detail in the previous chapter, other activities can also be identified as a bad habit. This, like most everything else, depends on the person you are. While one person can draw boundaries and says that an hour in front of the TV is good for him because he can switch off for a moment, another person is hooked by television: he consumes it all and leaves no room for the essential things. In general, however, increased television consumption is seen as negative.

In addition to the many methods that help you integrate new habits, replacing a bad habit directly with a good one works wonders. When you suddenly stop following a routine, it can throw you back into a bad way of thinking and acting. Fix the problem yourself and find a suitable replacement that also meets your needs!

If you want to eliminate a habit, you must fight against your natural instincts. If you set a goal to spend less money on shopping, it will be difficult at first. It is much easier to respond to the thing that triggers the desire to buy with something else that gives you a rewarding feeling. The trigger and the reward usually remain the same as long as you know what needs you are satisfying with the habit. In some cases, the desire for new clothes goes hand in hand with the need to boost self-esteem. Now, if someone who invests too much money in clothes sits in front of the computer, they are probably triggering this habit. However, you can now respond to this trigger by dressing up for yourself, which will also boost your self-confidence as a reward. In the same way, you can write a little letter to yourself.

In search of a good replacement for the habit, you need to try things out for yourself. By doing this, you will find out which activity satisfies your need, making you less likely to want to give in to your bad habit. Once you have found a good alternative, the key is to always do it when the trigger or need for a reward happens. At first, you'll find it a little easier because new activities reward us much more than the old habits could. The key to the process is to persevere. Helpful, practical tips will help you integrate it as a regular habit. You'll learn about these throughout the book. The more often you do your new habit, the more it feels like a routine until it just happens automatically after a while.

Ideas for Replacing Classic Habit Patterns

- **When you get cravings, do you reach for sweets straight away?**

  Humans sometimes find it difficult to distinguish between hunger and thirst. When you feel a sense of hunger or appetite, it's sometimes because your body needs fluids. How about drinking a glass of water next time so that your stomach is full? For others, chewing gum will help get rid of your appetite. A healthy snack, for example, nuts, vegetables, or sweet fruit, is also a super alternative to an unhealthy snack. Researchers have also found that scents can influence our appetite. For example, essential oils with an apple or raspberry aroma can stimulate your appetite for healthy fruit instead of unhealthy sweets.

- **Your coffee consumption knows no bounds?**

Too much caffeine is unhealthy and every adult probably knows that. Nevertheless, many tend to consume unhealthy amounts of coffee. Everywhere - at work, at the coffee shop, with friends, or at home - the body craves coffee. A super alternative if you feel this craving is green or black tea. These also contain caffeine, but these alternatives are bound to tannins. As a result, your body absorbs the caffeine more slowly and stores it longer. A cup of tea thus triggers the same effect in you as a cup of coffee. If you don't know a limit here, resort to other decaffeinated teas or coffee when a craving arises.

- **Do you look too much at your smartphone?**

This phenomenon is common in today's world. The flow of information, the social need, and the many small rewards with which, for example, mobile games addict consumers tempt them to reach for the smartphone regularly. In the process, the view of what is essential to real life is usually lost. Feelings of gratitude, happiness, and joy gradually diminish, causing consumers to fall into negative thought patterns. Every time you feel the urge to reach for your smartphone again, for example, due to stress, you look for an alternative that relaxes you: Mindfulness exercises, a short walk, a short reading break, or a cup of tea. It is also important not to let the temptation lie in the immediate vicinity. Instead, put your smartphone in the closet or in another room to avoid possible triggers such as messages or other distractions.

- **Do you stress your way through your daily routine?**

Getting out of bed early enough in the morning to complete your morning routine in peace is very difficult for a certain type of person. However, this often leads to you already being very stressed in the morning, which will likely continue throughout your daily life. Even though it is hard at the beginning, you should schedule enough time to start the day relaxed so that you can look back on it positively and even reduce the risk of heart rhythm disease by reducing stress. Get up a little earlier and perhaps do a little mindfulness exercise or meditation as well. In this way, you will also satisfy your need for relaxation in the morning. You will lower your stress level and start the new day directly with positive thoughts.

Focus on Your Improved Self

Your focus is the tool you need to use in restructuring your habits. But what does it actually mean to be focused?

Focused people direct their full attention to one thing of particular importance and recognize what they have to block and set aside to concentrate on the task at hand. It is not about pure concentration, which is necessary for the accomplishment of individual tasks, but about keeping one's goal or project present at all times. Each and every aspect of one's character and a wide range of behaviors are geared solely toward achieving the goal in question. So, you can be focused without putting in the necessary concentration, and in the same way, you can be focused without putting any attention on your task. In one day, it is possible to complete three projects with full concentration during working hours without having a fixed goal in mind. Thus, you work without focus. However, if you still sit down in the evening for a personal goal, you are focused but not necessarily concentrated.

In order to stay focused at all times, you need to have fixed goals in mind that you are passionate about and create a strategic plan to achieve them. First, however, you need to recognize your own priorities. The risk of losing your focus increases the more tasks you burden yourself with at the same time. What is the most important thing for you in your life? What brings you closer to happiness? These are things you need to figure out, and if possible, you should also find out which tasks are preventing you from achieving your goals. If you can, you should shift your attention to less important things and put them off, at least for the time being. . For more on this, take another look at the chapter "Learn to Say No." Being focused doesn't mean saying yes to everything that comes your way and permanently imposing new obligations on yourself all the time. Focus means saying "no" to things that paralyze you from restructuring.

Confucius, a well-known Chinese philosopher who taught two and a half thousand years ago, once said, *"If you hunt two rabbits at the same time, you won't catch either of them."*

We all know the feeling when the mountain of our own obligations has become so big that we don't dare approach or fulfill any of them wholeheartedly. We feel overwhelmed and lose our entire thought structure. However, there are several aspects and methods that can help you stay focused. These usually make use of strategic approaches because only a successful strategy will lead us to our desired goal.

1. Set Priorities

To ensure that you never lose your focus, it is essential to only set important goals that significantly increase your personal satisfaction. At the very most, set three goals for yourself at once and rank them in order of personal importance.

1. The first goal is essential for your quality of life.

2. The second goal is very important to you, but your quality of life is not directly linked to the implementation of the goal.

3. The third goal is logically important to you as well, but it is not difficult for you to do without it.

If you ever run out of energy, have too many things to do, or have a lot of stress at work or in your personal life, you can take action right away and put your focus on your most important goal. If you don't put your goals in order of how important they are to you, you might stop trying when you're too busy and just completely stagnate. However, goals are irreplaceable in the process of freeing your mind and revitalizing your body. We grow by doing things. Only by getting out of their comfort zone often does a person have a chance to become wise and strong. Consequently, his mind becomes stable enough to handle setbacks accordingly - as a lesson.

2. Remain Independent of Other Opinions

Dependence on the approval of others can benefit you in some cases as long as it creates healthy pressure within you. However, if you lose the balance between prioritizing yourself and the need to please everyone, you run the risk of losing yourself. You always come first: you are the person who decides how many tasks you need to accomplish (simultaneously). For this, it is important to make your own self-satisfaction independent of the opinions of others. For example, if you can't help a person because you are working on your goals and habits, that's fine. No one decides what you do except yourself.

Of course, interpersonal relationships are essential for us because we also need help, advice, or assistance from time to time. It is never a question of isolating yourself or foregoing the benefits of friendships, family, or partnerships which you naturally need to nurture just as much as the others. Nevertheless, someone may say something that demotivates or hurts you. In such moments, always keep in mind that no one knows everything. This person is arguing from a different perspective, based on different experiences than your personal opinion. In such moments, try to maintain focus on yourself, your insights, and your path. This will help you learn how to interpret the criticism accordingly. It can help you rise above yourself if you see it not as a personal attack but as well-meaning advice. As you process the criticism and realize that it is unjustified, you should not feel resentment, anger, or humility. Know and love yourself. Focus on your strengths and accomplishments to remain as independent from the opinions of others as possible and to motivate yourself to continue changing and discovering new paths. Stay true to yourself and your resolutions, and start building self-confidence. Work on yourself and start following your intuition more.

3. Write Down Your Goals

Do you remember situations like when you're shopping, and you thought, "I don't need a list, I can remember those few items," but ended up forgetting the most important things? You didn't focus properly because to do that seriously, you also need a written note regularly reminding you what you want to change. Every day we are confronted with a flood of news and information that our brains have to process, whether on TV, in the newspaper, via smartphone, or through conversations with others. You are constantly taking in new stimuli, which your brain filters automatically based on your habits and preferences. A new habit that your brain hasn't yet marked as a preference quickly becomes less important and can even be forgotten. Write down the new habits you want to add to your life, and if you can, try to remember them often, so you're always focused on yourself.

4. Reflect on Yourself

Not every habit change goes according to plan because sooner or later, you will face obstacles that are sometimes a lot harder to overcome. Even the paths of the happiest or the most successful people were uneven and rocky. Change always means small fights with yourself, which you can win with the proper focus and method.

Reflecting regularly on current progress, obstacles, and even past and future efforts keeps your objective in mind. Check whether you are still on the right path regularly, such as every weekend for half an hour or once a month, if that is too difficult at first. For detailed instructions on how to personally reflect on your own goals, see the chapter "Your Guide to Checking Your Progress."

5. Use Reminders

Even though the smartphone tends to promote negative thought patterns in many examples, it can also help you integrate new habits into your life. It's normal to get lost sometimes in the information jungle. You may remember your goal because you wrote it down, but it is easy to forget, especially in the beginning of implementation. There are apps that will remind you to do something at a time that you choose. Most smartphones come with this great feature right out of the box.

The reminders help you to regularly focus on the things that are important to you until they become second nature. Do you plan to go to bed earlier, for example? Always remind yourself at 10 p.m. to get ready for bed and go to sleep. If you don't know how to use a smartphone well, you can also ask someone you trust to remind you regularly of the new habit.

6. Gain Focus through Routines

Every change takes time to become a habit. It doesn't matter if these are new thought patterns that you learn through mindfulness exercises or if they are old habits like working out or watching what you eat because your body and mind are continuously learning. As soon as you do an activity or think in a certain way more often, it starts to get rid of other bad habits and makes things simpler. You will also find it easier to reach new goals and put them into action because your mind also learns how to deal with goals and changes, making it easier to integrate them into everyday life. Setbacks or moments of humility are normal and should not stop you from moving forward and growing. Only those who step out of their comfort zones have the chance to improve their lives significantly.

How to Overcome Setbacks

Most people long to change their behavior and realize that there will be setbacks along the way. Dealing with them is not easy, but the long-awaited success directly depends on the right way of handling it. Keep your mind on the habit change and keep working on it because a setback is more than the word "pauses." It trains you to deal with unwanted events and negative feelings.

Your brain is your strongest organ, which has memorized any behavioral patterns. First and foremost, you need to understand that habits work in order to find a way to deal with setbacks that will keep you motivated to follow through with the habit change. To do this, it is important to consider yourself as your best friend whom you treat with love, respect, and understanding – even during the bad times. You deserve exactly the same care. The top priority is always you. Start treating yourself with the same respect, love, and understanding as you do with your loved ones.

If you're aiming to change a habit, you can't rule out setbacks per se. Even though the point is to train yourself to use setbacks as learning opportunities, this still happens in the process. Your body and mind need time to consolidate patterns of action and thought. Having a bad day, meeting unfriendly people, or, in the worst case, losing a loved one can make you want to fall back into a pattern that you're trying to break.

Even if you slip back into an old pattern of behavior, continue to cherish yourself. Treat yourself with respect, love, and understanding because that is exactly what you need in a difficult phase! Suppose you fall into a negative pattern of thinking and put yourself down. In that case, something may happen that will ultimately turn you off from a habit change – you associate your goal, the good habit, with negative feelings which completely destroy your progress. Always focus on small goals and be proud of every success, no matter how small. Practice self-compassion, self-love, and patience with yourself!

Many studies show that setbacks are normal and won't stop you from making a new habit as long as you continue to give yourself positive encouragement. Get up and keep going as if nothing happened! At best, you might even learn more about yourself by figuring out what made you start the bad habit and what made you decide to break it. For example, if you want to eat better but a coworker brings a cake to work and you can't say no, think about how you can avoid this in the future. Bring a protein bar, some fruit, or a tasty, low-calorie drink just to be safe. In case a coworker offers tempting sweets again, having a healthy alternative to unhealthy snacks will take a lot of pressure off of you.

Define Fixed Goals

Without goals, we wander around aimlessly and our heads are filled with chaotic thoughts which stray us away from our path to happiness. Setting the right goals is essential if you want to improve yourself, strive for success, or seek personal happiness in life. But how exactly does this mechanism work? What makes fixed goals our inner compass?

"The aimless man suffers his fate, the purposeful man shapes it."

This quote comes from Immanuel Kant, who was very precise in recognizing his own scope for action. It describes that you are responsible for shaping your life according to your wishes. You are not powerless, no matter what happens to you – even the strongest and hardest strokes of fate give you a chance to grow. You have the opportunity to figure out how to deal with your sadness, anger, or even fear and turn these emotions into something positive: self-knowledge.

Those who have their goals firmly in mind become their own motivators. The inner drive to want to achieve something makes us get up every day – even if it's just going to work every day to earn money. Set your own standards and work on your own personal growth. Your life will become much easier to navigate: goals give you a sense of direction and push you to move up the steps of happiness. When you regularly look back on your life and celebrate the small wins you get from reaching small goals, you automatically feel more confident. Permanent self-improvement can even make you live longer. Happy and satisfied people give themselves many precious moments and a few years of life.

Another important factor is your individual motivation. People have a much harder time pursuing and reaching goals that were set for them by external sources, like an employer, parents, or a partner. A study conducted by researchers at the University of Pennsylvania found that people are more likely to form and integrate good habits if they set their own goals instead of having them predefined by other parties. Find your own goals that fit with who you are and help you reach your own idea of happiness. Ask about your ideas and needs in life and give them enough space even when you are looking for fixed goals.

Writing down your goals seems like a small effort, but it will lead you to you achieving your goals with a higher probability. This effect has also been proven scientifically because the pressure you put on yourself is significantly higher when you can see your goal and even feel it through the paper. At first, our own goals may overwhelm us because we tend to look for big solutions that promise us huge success right away. But the path to your goal is also an important factor in your growth process. Look for smaller goals and make a detailed plan for how to reach them. You will learn exactly how to proceed in the following chapters.

Rest easy because fixed goals don't mean you'll get there without deviation. Along the way, you'll get to know yourself better, which is why your own goals and making adjustments to them are a core element of personal improvement. Do you find that a goal doesn't meet your expectations or that you have something else in mind? This is a very important thing to realize. It helps you find yourself and figure out what you need.

Those who think about their goals often confront themselves with an inner emptiness. In society, he looks for ideals that seem to dictate his goals. Large, unattainable goals quickly follow, which do not correspond to who he is in any way. He can only disappoint himself. Learn to always recognize what your desires and needs are, and as a result, find the right intentions for yourself. The following chapters hold valuable information for you that will help you easily achieve future goals. Merge out feelings of humility and disappointment completely!

Your Delimitation of Small and Large Goals

Those who immediately set goals that are too big are quickly discouraged. Large goals overwhelm us, we don't know how to approach them, and we begin to resign. We quickly get caught up in negative thought patterns, so we rarely have the courage to change. Your self-esteem, personal satisfaction, and self-confidence suffer immensely. No change in behavior follows, and we continue our lives as before, with the same old habits and structures. Only one thing is different: we feel bad.

While it's easy to say to yourself that you want to achieve this or that in five years, only one thing makes these big, longed-for goals realistic: intermediate stages. You have to find your way! Define how you will achieve your big goal. The small, realistic goals make it easier for you to make that huge success you long for a reality. They influence your thinking pattern and strengthen your self-confidence, even if the goals are still so small. Then, you venture further and further into new areas and can expand your goals as soon as you have mastered each step. Every change, no matter how small, counts in this process. According to Gotthold Ephraim Lessing, "The slowest who does not lose sight of his goal still walks faster than the one who wanders without a goal."

There are different definitions of goals: daily goals, weekly goals, monthly goals, annual goals, or even goals that you want to achieve in several years. The smaller goals can always help get the bigger ones done. This way, you'll always know how to get to your biggest goal, and you'll be able to overcome every obstacle and reach all of your goals. Only by setting small goals every day, week, or month to your big goal can you get there and have a chance to reach it. Avoid being overwhelmed and prevent inner chaos through detailed paths to finally free yourself from negative thoughts!

Focus on your small goals and reward yourself regularly. You will automatically strengthen your self-confidence and motivation to strive for further goals. Small successes are essential for habit formation, as habit research also proves. So if you are striving for larger goals, you need to break them down into small ones so that you are regularly given successes that encourage you to change your habits from now on. In this way, you guarantee yourself an actual desired restructuring of your everyday life!

An Everyday Example

An ideal example is the desire to exercise regularly. Tired and hungry after work, many people find it difficult and lack the motivation to pack their sports bag and go to the gym or do a sports session at home. It's no surprise, given the enormity of the challenge. You have to invest a lot of time and finding motivation in times of exhaustion is something very few people manage to do. But even for this problem, there is a solution: for example, in order to achieve the larger goal of integrating sports into everyday life, you could first aim for smaller goals. First, start by putting the packed gym bag in your car. Even if you don't go to the gym that same day, you'll be one small step closer to your goal, no matter how small the activity.

Does this example seem a little strange to you? Try to think a few steps further, then you will understand what it means to you. After all, the smaller the steps, the less that stops you from performing the action. The next step is to make going to the gym easier for you. Once you get there, don't immediately aim to push through an hour. Start slowly and expand the new habit in stages. At first, you can also ride a bike or do a few exercises for 10 to

20 minutes. Nothing can stop you from working out longer if you still want to do it and your body and mind are motivated. However, if this mechanism works backwards and you decide to exercise for an hour but are exhausted after 20 minutes, you will go home disappointed even though you have made progress. This will make it harder for you to go to the gym again.

Automatically activate your reward system when you achieve even the smallest goals and take it a step further. Start celebrating your successes because they deserve to be celebrated. Always keep in mind that you are always moving forward, even if you are taking minimal steps. Eventually, automaticity will kick in. Going to the gym after work becomes a routine, something you do without thought, without consideration, and without fighting the urge to incorporate a new habit. A little tip worth its weight in gold when it comes to sports and other areas is to create liabilities! Find a workout partner, or give yourself fixed dates to keep you going.

Never Aimless Again: How to Find New Goals

When you begin to navigate the chaos of the world, a sense of aimlessness quickly sets in. Nowadays, you have thousands of options to satisfy all your needs directly. We begin to lose ourselves. There are temptations around every corner, but not all of them will get you to where you want to be in life. Self-reflection is an irreplaceable strategy to give your own personality the space it needs to flourish in this world. Follow your inner voice and regularly reflect to figure out your life's purpose. In order to grow, you need concrete, realistic, and attainable goals that suit you.

Everyone is allowed to make mistakes in the search for goals, but it is important to learn to accept them and find new ways that work better for you.

You, too, will experience that some goals did not quite fit your expectations. Regardless of the fact that you should avoid big goals – which was explained to you extensively in the previous part of this chapter – there are also some wrong decisions. This is no cause for grief. On the way to your inner self, it is normal to err. It even holds something good for you: self-knowledge. You find more and more ways to be happy and to be yourself because you get to know your needs. This is a real blessing in this chaotic and fast-moving world.

Let's go one step further: it's about your personal drive. In order for you to achieve something, it is important to desire change from the bottom of your heart. Only those who are honest with themselves and their emotions will find the discipline necessary to realize their desires. Of course, a person who has not played sports for a long time would not want to at first, but that is not the point in this context. Instead, the point is that this person also knows the benefits of physical exercise. Perhaps she wants to lose weight and can find the inner drive through it. The inner need to suffer less pain from being overweight or to fit into her favorite jeans again drives her.

For self-discovery purposes - on a professional level, for example - there are internships and other areas that you can try out that will help you get to know yourself better and figure out what needs drive you personally. The adage "The proof of the pudding is in the eating!" applies in full. Want to free your mind? Start pushing past your own limits. This will only work if you regularly move out of your comfort zone and pick up activities that are outside of your usual habits. You'll be able to do this when you start putting your goals into action. The first step, however, is to find them. These four effective methods will help you do that. Get to know your needs and find goals that fit your personality with ease.

1. Reflect on Your Areas of Life

Do you want to find out what you are really striving for? Then start by taking a closer look at your own life and the path to your current starting point. Of course, this doesn't mean wallowing in the past and mourning it, but reflecting on which steps and moments you remember positively and which ones you look back on "negatively." Both variations serve as a great lesson in how to define happiness.

Your current life situation offers a great opportunity to question your own needs. Look at different areas of your life, both private and professional. On a private level, for example, the following aspects are relevant:

- one's spirituality or religion

- family relationship patterns

- love

- your friendships

- your hobbies and all activities you pursue in your free time

- the personal drive for further education (reading, learning, etc.)

- your internal and external order

- your diet

- physical workout (sports)

- your sleep behavior

- your thought structures

Continue to analyze yourself on a professional level:

- What is the working atmosphere like?

- Are you appropriately challenged, under-challenged, or over-challenged at work?

- Do you have growth potential in your work?

- How is your relationship with your superiors?

- Do your colleagues and employer value your work appropriately?

- How do you rate your work itself?

- Are you satisfied with your financial situation?

By actively dealing with different areas of your life, including the past and present, you gain the opportunity to figure out where you want to make changes. Find out what you want from each area and how you can take small, achievable steps toward your big goal. Do you find an opportunity for growth or a lack thereof? Then here is your chance to set a new goal for yourself.

Reflecting on your behavior is also a small but perfect solution when searching for yourself. Ask yourself what roles you take on situationally: who are you at work, with your family, with friends, or with your partner? In which role do you feel most comfortable, and how can you use this in other areas of your life? Write down your ideas and thoughts so that you can remember them and they don't get lost. You can question your entire life in stages. Don't try to do too much at once. For example, you could start by spending 10 or 20 minutes privately thinking about how you feel about your family relationships or your friendships.

The Plus and Minus Analysis of Your Life

Not everyone recognizes right away what makes them happy and what harms them. Tasks quickly pile up. You begin to pursue activities that have nothing to do with who you are at all. Your mind becomes increasingly sluggish and you lose sight of who you are. Finally, you can find a way out! There is a great way to bring out more of the good things in life. The first step is to recognize what they are in the first place. In the next step, you start to reduce negative and burdensome aspects based on your own range of actions.

Take a moment for yourself in a quiet place where you feel comfortable. Now, note all the things in your life that trigger positive feelings in you and those that you currently perceive as burdensome or negative. Explain why you feel this way and find out what your opinion is based on. It is helpful to rank all positive aspects according to personal relevance so that you can work out your priorities in life. The plus and minus analysis will help you to do this. Make a list of both enriching and burdening influences in your life.

Possible Pluses:

- love ones or things

- hobbies or preferences

- previous successes

- everything you are grateful for in life

- met needs

- anything that gives you pleasure or makes you happy

- things that make you laugh

- everything that is important to you

Possible Minus Points:

- activities that you have to comply with but do not want to

- things that often trigger anger in you

- strokes of fate or stressful circumstances that you have not yet found a good way to deal with

- different types of personally perceived problems

- anything that triggers inner pain or sadness in you

- things that promote negative stress in you

- people with whom you cannot get along well

With the plus and minus analysis, you can find out where change is necessary for you. This also concerns how you handle the minuses and the pluses. A possible goal could be that you want to put more focus on those things that you consider positive. For example, if time in nature gives you a lot of strength and this is one of the positive points in your life, then make it a goal to set a day aside every two weeks for yourself to enjoy nature to the fullest.

Your Perfect Day

Another great way to identify your needs is to let your imagination run wild. Indulge yourself and try to imagine your perfect day. There are no limits to what you can do. These will only come into play as you progress and derive realistic goals from your imagination.

Take something to write with and a little quiet time to yourself. Put on some relaxing music or light some candles to create a pleasant atmosphere. Now, think about what your perfect day would look like. Fix each thought in writing to get the best possible result from the exercise later. The method helps you expand your action and thinking to overcome self-imposed limits. Imagine whatever you want. What have you already achieved that day? What would you like to do with which people?

Be sure to fill the entire day and make sure that at no point could a feeling of boredom creep in. Look for small details such as the landscape, the weather, the décor of the rooms you'll be in on your perfect day, the people around you, and how you will interact with them. Even the animals or plants that are there may have more significance later.

Think about what activities you are pursuing. Are you perhaps even at work for a while because in your imagination, you are pursuing another job, or maybe you are working on other projects that are personally beneficial or fulfilling to you? What hobbies do you pursue, what is your financial situation, and what material possessions do you have there?

On your perfect day, you can also describe things that are already in your life. It can be people, your favorite book, or a piece of clothing you like to wear that makes you feel grateful for everything that has great value to you. With this exercise, you begin to think broader and bigger. We tend to think and set goals within our limits, some of which we set ourselves. In many cases, these boundaries don't even exist except in our minds. When we begin to mentally overcome them, we expand our options on what to do many times over. Of course, if you are aiming for big goals and recognize them with the help of the exercise, you need to set small stages and break this big goal down into small, realistic goals first. This will also bring you a step closer to what you have in mind at a time without stagnating.

How do you now derive realistic goals from your perfect day and recognize which aspects are particularly important to you?

1. What was indispensable for you on that day? Which aspect of the day would make you particularly sad unless you could turn it into reality?

2. Which aspects are important to you, and which could you do without in case of doubt?

3. What about the perfect day was a beautiful aspect and brought you joy but is not crucial to your happiness?

Try to divide your day into these three categories and derive what really counts for you in life. In this way, you can gradually determine your goals. For example, did you spend your perfect day outside? Then your body may be craving the outdoors. A realistic goal now might be to spend more time there. Did you enjoy spending time with a certain person on your perfect day? Then it may be time to give that person more time in your life. Did you wear colorful clothes, something you tend to avoid in your personal life? Start bringing color into your life in the real world and let your happiness shine from the inside out. Don't take on too much at once in the beginning. Take small steps, and start aiming for the most important goals in stages!

It makes sense to repeat this exercise at regular intervals because you are in the process of further development. As you change, so do your needs and desires, which is why you also need new goals on a regular basis that will lead you to your personal happiness.

Your 80th Birthday

To avoid inner conflicts, your goals must be in harmony with your values. Many people are actually unaware of what values and morals are important to them. This exercise will help. Get to know yourself and find out which values are important to you personally. Knowing your values allows you to formulate new, individual goals easily. In this exercise, you will look at your entire life from a new perspective.

To do this, imagine that there is a big party in your honor for your 80th birthday. You are the center of attention – all the guests want to congratulate you and talk to you while you enjoy eating your birthday cake on a comfortable armchair.

After everyone has eaten their birthday cake together, perhaps had a cup of coffee or tea to go with it, four people give a speech for and about you. It is about everything you stood for, what you have achieved, and your endearing personal qualities. These four people are:

- a family member,

- your most important boyfriend or girlfriend,

- one of your former work colleagues, and

- a person from the municipality or city where you live.

In your mind, what would these four people say about you? Try to overcome your limitations here and do not focus too much on your current situation. It is not about what these people would say about you in the present reality but exclusively about who you would like to be. In doing so, you are trying to answer how you want other people – who have played a key role in your life so far – to remember you.

Many people look back on the last days of their lives and feel sad about what they didn't do or what they would have liked to have done differently. This exercise works preventively so that you can look back at the end of your life with as few negative upsets as possible.

Now how does this exercise relate to your inner value system? The statements of the people giving a speech about you contain your individual positive qualities. Were you a person who always said what you thought and/or did you help other people a lot? Then, honesty and helpfulness are those values that have meaning for you.

Through these values, you can derive new goals for yourself. For example, at an older age, you could say that you like to help others more, perhaps by volunteering or giving more to a loved one like your mother.

While you can identify your personal values and formulate new goals here, aligning previously established goals with them is equally important. An inner struggle and conflict will keep you to a standstill. We begin to sabotage ourselves in the implementation. Prevent this from happening by making sure that your goals are always in line with your values.

Finding Motivation Through the Right Formulation of Goals

How you formulate goals and what goals you set strongly influence whether or not you can turn them into reality. Goal setting has tremendous power that can gradually improve your life if it is realistic and in alignment with who you are.

Once you resolve to strive for change, you need to set small (stage) goals that, when successfully achieved, will give you the confidence to take further steps toward an improved life. Keep your goals in writing and preferably present in a place you cross daily. Instinctively, this will multiply your inner drive. Many people fail to make the changes they long for because they don't align their goals with their values and needs or are overwhelmed with big goals. And yet another factor that hinders implementation is goal formulation. You should write down the change you long for as soon as you set your sights on it. It is undoubtedly difficult to find the right words. Language is powerful, and so is writing. It can motivate us, delight us, or hinder us and make us sad. All emotions resonate. Therefore, this book will teach you which aspects can help you keep your inner emotional world motivated and happy so that you can achieve any goal. Now, let's go through each individual aspect together.

Formulate Positive Goals

Especially when it comes to breaking a bad habit, we usually set the goals in a negative way, like saying, "I don't want to watch so much TV anymore." However, it's hard for your brain to understand as it can hardly accept this information and cannot process negative goals. Just thinking about a habit you've had for a long time helps you keep doing it. It is much better for your brain to accept positive goals and follow up your words with actions. Therefore, always avoid the little word "don't" and naming the bad habit when setting a new goal. In the example given, you could look for an alternative and set it as a positive call to action for yourself, like saying, "I want to read more in the evening."

Studies have proven many times that we are more likely to achieve goals when we set a desired outcome rather than trying to eliminate a bad habit. The reason is that the presence of negative goals makes you feel incompetent, and as a result, weakens your self-confidence. You are less likely to focus on your personal progress. Even if a change in behavior occurs, you hardly feel any effect on your individual satisfaction. You block all positive thought patterns. Stop fighting a battle against yourself and start affirming yourself! Positive goals are followed by significant change. You immediately motivate yourself to integrate a new habit instead of a bad one.

Set a Time

Scheduled goals create a framework that triggers the necessary pressure in you to take action. Setting goals on a schedule gives you a framework that pushes you to take action. Write down when you want to reach your goal, just like you would in a contract. Most of the time, oral agreements are not good. Most people forget them as soon as an exciting event occurs. Think about what's possible when you give yourself a deadline! You could even make small buffers to help you feel better about the change. The deadline will motivate you to take action every day, bringing you closer and closer to your goal. Schedule the small intermediate steps in between and set dates for when you will reach 25, 50, 75, and 100 percent of your goal! The smaller the intervals are, the more structure you create within yourself.

Not meeting your deadline? That's okay, too. While deviations shouldn't be the rule, you'll need a little time in the beginning to learn how to allocate your energy. Nevertheless, always set a time because a goal without a deadline runs the risk of never being achieved. In essence, it is an intention rather than a goal. Unlike goals, an intention makes you manipulate yourself. You keep putting things off until the following day, losing motivation and self-confidence. You stop believing your words. Consider yourself lucky because you now know what separates an intention from an actual goal, unlike most people. Start today and think about when you want to improve your life a little bit!

Feel Your Goals

You should feel strongly about a goal you have set. Because only behind the goals formulated with passion lies true motivation. Choose your words wisely and consider what feelings they should evoke. Awaken a fire within you with which you passionately strive for your goal!

It helps you visualize what will occur once you reach your goal. For example, are you planning a set exercise routine? Imagine how stronger and more energetic you will be after the first few weeks.

Put all your wishes and ideas in writing, and resort to emotionally charged words. Energize your mind, and motivate yourself to do something every day to improve your current state! The more specific you are in describing your goal and state, the easier it will be to measure. Describe in detail how your life will change. The following questions will help you describe exactly what positive impact implementing the goal will have on you:

- What occurs once you reach your goal?

- How are you changing personally?

- How will your (social) environment change?

- What changes have occurred externally when you achieve your goal (for example, remodeling a room in your home)?

- How will your circle of acquaintances react to your success?

- What changes that are not outwardly apparent occur once you reach your goal (for example, emotional stability)?

Always answer these questions in the past tense, for example, "I will have read three books by January 1 next year". When you say things like "I will," "I should," "I have to," or "I would like," you make it harder to get things done. The terms suggest that you might not be able to achieve the goal. If you believe in yourself, you will be an enormous step closer to achieving your goals.

In addition, a short list of bullet points can also help you keep track of the important parts of the goal. Here, you briefly summarize your goal and set a deadline for when you want to achieve it.

If you have more than one goal at the same time, prioritize them. As soon as you notice that you have taken on too much, you can directly identify the most important goal and disregard the others for the time being.

Document Your Progress

When you travel, you decide on a time to reach your destination. You decide how to get there, pick the most suitable route, see if there are any delays, and consider how to change your route if traffic jams or other obstacles block your way. On the road, you can permanently check if you are on the right track and correct the route if necessary.

Even personal goals that don't necessarily have anything to do with a trip need regular progress monitoring. Studies have proven that reflecting on your goals and the entire writing process increases the likelihood of actually achieving them. You reflect on your journey, consider where adjustments are needed, and respond directly when obstacles arise. This method is used in project management, software development, and many other professional fields. It is a true miracle tool. Make this method your own, too, and benefit from an inner structure and increased motivation when implementing your goals:

1. In the first step, you draw a horizontal axis for this, which records your starting point on the left side and the complete implementation of your goal on the right side. Thus, the entire axis is your path to the goal.

2. Next, look at where you currently stand. How far have you already gone?

3. Now, compare your current situation with your defined stage goals. Are you where you wanted to be, are you already closer to your goal than planned, or have you not yet reached the intermediate steps?

4. You now have a chance to make adjustments. For example, how can you make a bigger leap to get a little closer to the milestone goal? Or have your schedules changed, so you have less capacity? Insofar as something changes in your life, your goals must change as well. Just plan a little more time! Time deferrals are occasionally useful. Nevertheless, you should not rest on regularly postponing your goal because your motivation and inner drive might suffer.

During the progress review, you have the chance to reflect on all external and internal circumstances. How are your mind and body coping with the changes? Do you feel that this goal continues to meet your needs and values, or is it time for an adjustment in goal setting? Aspects that have changed in your life independent of this goal – such as pregnancy, a new job, or a new relationship – also play into this, as your time may be significantly reduced as a result. In any case, it's better to adjust goals, push back deadlines, or prioritize other goals than to lose your passion and will. It helps you to self-reflect at all times. For progress monitoring of your personal goals, the following aspects serve as inspiration:

- your previous successes on the way to your goal

- your mental capacities

- the previous time and effort

- the steps still to be taken

- your available time

- external environmental changes

- your values

- the past and future costs (if any)

- The times set for your goal and the stages on the way there

Of course, you can also consider other aspects that are important to you when checking your progress. Take a moment in a pleasant environment where your mind can relax. In this process, treat yourself as a beloved friend who is allowed to make mistakes and experience the occasional setback. Self-love, self-compassion, and self-acceptance are incredibly important – at all times. Always focus on what you've done well so far and praise yourself regularly, preferably in writing. Start rewarding yourself for your successes with things or activities you enjoy. Immediately boost your serotonin and dopamine release, which directly puts your mind in a positive mood and associates the new habit or goal with a good feeling. You condition yourself to be more motivated and focused toward your goal. Nature has given us an incredible number of gifts: positive feelings, the chance to grow, bright and glorious colors, and our intelligence.

We are blessed with having friendships and relationships and access to an incredible amount of information that allows us to continually educate ourselves. Accept these gifts with gratitude and make the most of them! Small actions can make your mind and body feel good. It's quite a small effort to regularly reflect on your successes and goals in writing when you think of the myriad of benefits that come with it.

Kaizen: Your Japanese Formula for Success

Everywhere, society confronts people with the term "innovation." It stands for quick success through big changes and implies that behind every career of success lie big goals, big steps, and fast growth. However, the opposite is true. If you think big, you naturally boost your creativity and may even be able to grow quickly – the problem with this is that the longed-for successes are quickly lost with an increased probability. A major car manufacturer also had to go through this experience. Toyota, which was known for good quality, increased its production by 3 million cars in a short time. A great success, right? The customers saw it differently. In fact, the condition of the cars sold was much worse because the suppliers could no longer provide the same quality. As a result, Toyota had to recall 9 million cars, damaging its own reputation. The big change and the big goals led to the fact that the car manufacturer recorded regressions and had to pay a lot of money in the end. The entire process was not adapted to such a big change.

Even if you are dealing with the issue of habit change, big steps are very risky. You have experienced this several times in the course of the book. Think of many different examples which illustrate that sustainable success depends on small, realistic steps that can be easily integrated into life:

- radical diets

- hard work out plans

- acutely discard addictions

- strict savings plans

- get over being shy through exposure to uncomfortable social situations

- short trips with the partner to improve the relationship

These are just a few examples which show that big steps carry risks, such as yo-yo effects with a radical diet. The intense pressure, the rapid exhaustion, and the stress that comes with it can hardly be compensated for by the initial euphoria. You probably have quick wins at first, yet the old patterns creep in afterward, making you feel like a failure and less likely to make more changes. People are impatient and want to get results quickly, which is why they usually take on more than they can actually handle. All their energy goes into a single goal, so they quickly drip with exhaustion. Self-optimization and habit change, however, is not a sprint. Our life is a perpetual marathon, for which it is necessary to divide our energy reserves accordingly.

Whether Far Eastern or even in the West, habits play a significant role everywhere. This goes so far that there are concepts dedicated exclusively to this topic. They promise success and happiness. And indeed, these methods are real miracle cures, especially the Kaizen method. This philosophy of life and work originated in Japan and is used in many companies. It is probably the most popular method when it comes to changing habits or structures. It is popular on a personal and corporate level and even in government institutions. Translated, the method stands for a change for the better (*Kai* = change, *Zen* = for the better).

On a corporate level, it is the most important pillar for remaining competitive in the long term. Here, all employees and employers are given a voice, even the seemingly small intern. Everyone is allowed to criticize work processes, so teamwork is directly strengthened. Employees feel that they are an important part of a larger whole. Employees look at the entire company from every perspective, so all parties benefit exclusively.

Likewise, all employees and employers try every day to minimally improve internal processes in order to arrive at optimal solutions in the long term. This saves costs, materials, and time, then identifies and eliminates weak points and ensures long-term quality. If problems arise in the process, the companies have an immediate opportunity to rectify them before they seriously impact operations.

This treatment is a miracle and a cure for everyone, including you. It has led many people to success and personal happiness, as they have defined it individually. The advantages of the method are many:

- It defines realistic, simple, and actionable goals.

- Big goals get precision from small, simple steps.

- They eliminate the classic fears of failure.

- Your everyday life is minimally reshaped so that you hardly notice it.

- You activate your reward system through small successes.

- In the process, you automatically learn self-discipline.

- They promote all positive habits.

- Like companies in the marketplace, you can respond directly to problems.

- They learn to be self-reflective.

- The method is minimal as it requires little preparation, effort, and no special prior knowledge.

- You learn how to allocate your resources.

- You save an incredible amount of time by optimizing simple tasks.

This method is especially interesting for those people who are afraid of their own failure or perhaps have already had to experience one or two failures in radical habit changes and feel discouraged. In this chapter, learn about the Japanese success strategy. Learn how to adopt it and thereby continuously improve your life without internal pressure and fear of failure.

The Success Strategies of the Kaizen Method

"A journey of 1,000 miles begins with a single step."
- **Laozi, a Chinese philosopher from the 6th Century BC.**

Kaizen is an optimization philosophy that greatly resonates among the population, both companies and individuals. This is probably due to the fact that we live in an uncertain world, which is constantly changing and demands this very change from all members of society. But if you have to adapt permanently, you need a good strategy that leaves reserves of strength for everyday challenges.

To get started with Kaizen, hardly anything is needed at the beginning. A pen and a sheet of paper are enough to integrate the method into your life successfully. In this paper, create a rough plan of how you want to achieve your goals. In order to apply the method successfully, you should first clarify what you would like to improve. Then you will find the appropriate measures with which you can sustainably master the implementation. At its core, the Kaizen method makes use of ten brilliant tools:

- Continually question your current behavior.

- It is not about perfection but the constant search for process optimization.

- Empower yourself with new information.

- Take small and concrete steps to conserve your personal resources.

- Filter out where the cause of your problems lies.

- Adjust your measures directly as soon as (small) problems occur.

- Lay out a detailed plan.

- Define realistic goals.

- Remain open to incentives or criticism from others.

The Kaizen method also teaches us to always focus on the small, gradual changes that occur at the habit level. These should be as easy to implement as possible, so your everyday life hardly changes. You can achieve great things if you give 1% more each week than you did the previous. Just think about where you could be within a year. Do you want to eat healthier? Eat a small piece of fruit every day and skip an unhealthy snack in return. Would you like to exercise more? For starters, go for a five-minute walk during the day or once a week. Focus on the small changes and successes. The following week, eat a little more or use less sugar in your coffee. The list of ways you can slowly change your diet is incredibly long. Listen to your inner voice that communicates your individual needs. At no time should you feel like you need to restrict yourself.

This can be applied to many areas. We often start with something and realize that it does not bring us the desired satisfaction of our needs. Kaizen gives you the space you need for such realizations because change is always a process. Do you notice during the process that you are unhappy with it? Stop agonizing and find new goals and new patterns to integrate into your life. Do you enjoy something more than you thought you would and go into the desired habit? Simply integrate it more fully into your life. At any point in time, it's all about your personal needs and desires. When developing your individual plan, it is important to describe it in as much detail as possible. Address internal and external stimuli, your needs, your daily routine, and any situations in which you want to integrate the new habit. Schedules are also an important component here. At what time would you like to perform the new activity, and by when would you like to have implemented what percentage of the process?

As you and your daily structures change, you continue to find new goals or recognize how to adjust your goals in the short or long term to keep your desires at the forefront. Again, your larger goals are broken down into small, realistic goals that form a long-term plan. Big steps or hair-pulling solutions usually overwhelm us. Very few people are so disciplined that it is not difficult for them to completely change their daily routine. How these people manage it remains a mystery. On the other hand, most complain about demotivation, quick dropouts, fear of failure, pressure, and the problem of integrating new habits into their daily lives, which hardly change in structure. Think of the Toyota example here. Of course, you can plan to do an hour of sports every day. However, integrating sports into an old daily structure is more torture than choice. It's a matter of when you'll stop yourself from going back to the gym after work, eating later, having less time for your eve-ning relaxation rituals, or sleeping later. It's a gigantic hurdle. You need a large stockpile of energy reserves to overcome this hurdle, but this will be used up after a short time. Therefore, start slowly and go for a 15-minute walk, complete 5 minutes of gymnastic exercises, ride your bike to work one day a week, or schedule some time on the weekend to move your body. Over time, your body and mind will automatically adjust, making you really want to move.

How to Successfully Integrate the Kaizen Method into Your Life

All the information is of little use as long as you lack the knowl-edge for practice. How does this method become a part of your life? Self-reflection, plans, goals – all these terms can initially seem a bit overwhelming. But don't worry! Kaizen is a process. No one expects perfection. The further you get away from the idea of having to be perfect, the more likely you are to find perfection in the smallest everyday things.

Kaizen is a simple and helpful method that you can implement in just six steps:

1. Actively seek opportunities and goals that involve improvement!

2. Research ideas, methods, and approaches that will bring you closer to your goal. Here, the perspective of outsiders is also an inspiring source.

3. Break your goal down into small steps and small results!

4. Plan how and when you can achieve each small result without making major changes to your daily routine or drawing heavily on resources elsewhere!

5. Continually review your progress and adjust timelines, measures, or your interim goals as needed!

6. Find a new target!

In the routine and continuous process, your mind and body will adjust more and more to the changes. Depending on the nature of your personality, it is more or less easy for you to change something in your life, especially in the beginning. Yet, we humans need change, we have merely unlearned it. But just as you can learn new languages over time, your body and mind learn how change works in the process. You begin to crave new influences and structures quite automatically over time.

In the comfort of everyday life, we often don't seek change without the necessary incentive. Apparently, everything works. The problem with this is that we become dull, our minds become sluggish, and over time we become dissatisfied without knowing the cause. The cause is clear – we are bored because we are trapped in our everyday life. We start grabbing new possessions and chasing bargains just to feel something for a short moment. It seems as if something has changed, but after a few hours, the same feeling returns.

The longer you stick to your comfortable habits and stay in your comfort zone, the harder it is to overcome inner inertia and explore new areas, even if you are aware of the benefits, positive feelings, new experiences, and impressions. Start to leave this zone regularly, even if it's only once a month at first. You can change the way you work, try new food, go out partying properly for a change, try a new hairstyle, approach strangers, or explore a new place. Keep this intention in mind and write it in your diary to make a commitment. Think carefully about what you want to do and when you will do it. Write down all the important information on a post-it, which you will find every day on your mirror, calendar, or notebook. The more detailed your plan is, the more likely you are to put it into action.

The Five Basic Principles of the Kaizen Method

When you start using the great techniques of the Kaizen method, it helps to stick to the five basic principles. They create a rough framework that gives structure in both professional and private contexts. You, too, can use these principles to feel positive effects in your everyday life immediately.

Standardization:

You keep trying things out, start integrating small changes into your everyday life, and then have the chance to see whether they bring you the success you long for. If it becomes clear that this behavior is good for you, you establish it as a standard and integrate it firmly into your everyday life. Once you have successfully integrated the new habit, start striving for something new to improve.

Critique Orientation:

Try to be open to new suggestions and criticism at all times throughout the process. Ask for it explicitly in one situation or another. See it as an opportunity to improve yourself continuously.

Quality Orientation:

Set your own standard of quality by deciding what you think a good life looks like. Try to apply this to your entire life and to all of your goals so that you can adjust your behavior accordingly through small, slow steps in a continuous process.

Process Orientation:

The more often you strive for change, the easier and more routinized it will be in the future. Meanwhile, you learn what you need and how to achieve your goals best – improve not only yourself but also every single change process. Gain control over your life!

If the process is improved, the results are automatically optimized as well. Do you sense that an undesirable outcome is occurring? No need to worry, using a simple process adjustment, you can improve every result and eliminate all problems. That's why it's also important to constantly analyze and optimize the process of any actions, goal realizations, or the like.

Self-Reflection as a Learning Element

The Kaizen method enables you to fully exploit all your potential and sustainably improve your environment and your entire life. However, continuous development and the integration of new habits require a little bit of self-commitment. This consists of regularly reflecting on your goals and path to bring out the best in yourself. Always remember who you are doing this for and why: so you can finally find the happiness you deserve. You'll start to feel positive effects on all kinds of levels, in terms of:

- your awareness,

- your physical and mental health,

- your creativity,

- your handling of stress, and

- your emotional intelligence.

After only a short time, you will feel better. All the feelings of success that this method gives you are pure balm for your soul.

Get to know yourself from the perspective of a friend: you take distance from yourself, your habitual patterns, and your emotions, and are much better able to make changes that contribute to your personal satisfaction. In doing so, you continually practice self-love and self-compassion. Set aside the pressure of living up to everything once and for all. Before you begin, take a step back: analyze your current habits using the W questions:

- What habits would you like to change?

- How exactly does the habit work?

- Where do you perform the habit?

- Why do you perform the habit/what are possible triggers?

- How do you feel while performing the habit?

- Who participates in the habit (e.g., partner)?

- What obstacles might you encounter?

- What habit do you want to follow/what is your goal?

- How can the goal be broken down into the smallest possible stages?

Ask yourself these questions, and more if necessary, to uncover the mechanism of a behavior at its core and to identify the causes and effects that will help you integrate a new habit. For example, if a bad habit is about a social need, then that need should continue to be met by other behaviors.

The search for new goals requires a precise, detailed description. Let's take the topic of sports as an example. Do you want to integrate sports into your life? That's a great approach. However, it leaves a lot open because sports can be practiced in many different ways, with or without people, and for many different reasons. If you resolve to do more sports, ask accordingly:

- Why do you want to exercise (e.g., strengthen your muscles, improve your endurance or flexibility, improve your posture, lose weight...)?

- What small activities could you incorporate into your life to achieve your goal (e.g., five minutes of yoga to become more limber)?

- Do you perform the activity alone or with other people?

- On which days and at what time would you like to perform the activity?

- When do you want to achieve which goals (e.g., after one month, get one centimeter lower with your hands while bending down)?

Again, you can digress further and ask yourself as many questions as you need to define your goals accurately. The more precise, the better! If you are clear about every little detail of your goals, it will be much easier to find the necessary actions. Without loss, without a sense of abandonment or humility, you'll begin to integrate the habit into your life not just for the short term but for the long term. Find your own focus, and you'll get closer and closer to who you are!

As soon as you start to slowly integrate the new behaviors into your life and move closer to your goals in stages, you should always monitor and reflect on them as well. Especially in the beginning, your body and mind will resist a bit because you have conditioned them to behave differently. In this way, your body has formed its links of situation, behavior, and reward. Changing these takes a little time. Self-examination is a key element of the Kaizen method. It helps you keep a desired behavior present in your mind. You'll never forget that you wanted to ride your bike or do your five-minute workout once a week. Having a small list or calendar where you check off the activity as soon as you've done it will remind you of the new habit at all times, even when the initial euphoria fades. Maintain control of your actions and a long-term view of your successes. Start motivating yourself right away by keeping a permanent eye on the process.

To optimize even the smallest of tasks and train yourself to be mindful, start by reflecting on the positive and negative changes in an activity you want to do every week. Let's take the topic of jointness as an example. Logically, you have to first define your goal. In a year, for example, you want to be able to do the splits. For this goal, you need measures and intermediate goals that you must complete repeatedly within the year. Of course, this is only a rough estimate. If you lose sight of yourself for too long, you will only be able to assess your body to a limited extent. The next step is to set the necessary intermediate goals. For this, you could decide that you want to be one to three centimeters lower in the splits after a month. How? By stretching for five minutes every day. Each evening, you reflect briefly:

- Did you perform the action/measure today?

- What did you find positive about the measures?

- What negative aspects did you perceive?

- How could you adjust your process to benefit more from the positive effects and eliminate the negative aspects if possible?

At the end of the week, look at the process as a whole:

- How much further are you compared to last week?

- How has the week been so far?

- Were the (daily) adjustments helpful, and did they optimize the process?

- How do you feel mentally?

- How do you feel physically?

- How much closer are you to your interim goal?

- Are the timeframes in which you want to achieve your goals realistic, or do they need adjustment?

This form of reflection is called a "sprint" in the Kaizen philosophy. You get a big step closer to your goal by regularly adjusting the process – just like a sprint. The small successes you celebrate weekly or even daily foster your inner enthusiasm for ongoing change and performance-oriented thinking in a positive sense. Performance is based on the pressures you often face in society. Instead, it's based on how you define it: you set your goals and believe in yourself throughout the process! Notice whether the goals seem to make sense for your personal satisfaction and individual growth or whether they are those imposed by society that you have adopted. Assess yourself and see if you notice any positive changes in yourself, for example, in terms of your self-perception. Find out your needs and interests and use the Kaizen method to fulfill your happiness. Step by step, you will develop your own life strategy, which will help you overcome any problems and grow steadily.

When people use the Kaizen method, they usually start by optimizing their physical and health aspects. The things that first come to mind when it comes to personal habits include sleeping patterns, getting enough exercise, or dietary changes. The main thing is to get started. In the process of changing your habit, you also get to know yourself emotionally because you reflect on your emotional world. The process automatically encourages you to engage further with your soul. This is your chance to have a well-tuned and balanced mind. Find out what makes you happy and what factors are important to you personally. Learn about your needs, nature, and environment, and keep these things in mind.

How to Learn from Your Mistakes

Everyone makes mistakes, including you, me, and all the people you have already met along the way. Anyone who thinks they never make mistakes and already know everything they need to know is obviously wearing blinders. He blocks his view from any form of self-criticism and, consequently, his chances of growth. In our world, there is a lot of information, some of which is helpful and some of which is not. It's not easy to figure out what our personal interests are, but we have the chance to improve ourselves and use as much information as possible to fulfill our purpose and personal satisfaction. It is your responsibility to get the input you need. The list of ways to inspire yourself and expand your knowledge is endless, whether it's books, lectures, magazines, or consultations with professionals. For example, you can start by consuming media consciously and actively. What aligns with your values? What knowledge appeals to you? What topics could you research further? Find the information that fits with who you are and what you're interested in. Watch talks by experts on YouTube or TED Talks, attend seminars, or start reading for five minutes every day. Other people's points of view are invaluable for your self-development because they expand your horizons of thought and give you new incentives to change your life for the better.

Another way to use our potential and develop ourselves is to converse with other people. Every person has had different experiences, read different books, and has their own knowledge that they've put together for themselves. This knowledge can inspire other people. Other points of view, new ideas or constructive criticism are priceless because they can move us forward, provided that we take them seriously and recognize the opportunity to improve. To do this, it is important to be open to criticism, incentives, and mistakes.

The most likely person to be happy and have a balanced mind is the one who learns to look at his mistakes as lessons and adjusts his goals, desires, and path to his fulfillment based on those changes. It is important – for oneself, as well as for one's loved ones – to have compassion, to allow mistakes, and to seek opportunities for personal growth from them. In this situation, it's important to start reflecting on these situations and how you can avoid making the same mistake in the future: what triggered it? Analyze all of the possible factors that could have been important in this case so that you can act immediately and take measures that can fix or even eliminate the root causes.

What is great about the Kaizen method? It's the fact that you can't cause any serious problems when changing your everyday structure because you don't take any acute measures and gradually integrate them into your life instead. It is exclusively about small, hardly noticeable changes. Consequently, small steps only allow for small problems you can fix directly by adjusting your goals, timing, or intermediate stages. In this way, you avoid feelings of failure, anxiety, demotivation, or exhaustion. You learn to reflect on yourself and train yourself to deal with mistakes or problems that may even go beyond a personal level. A structure is almost automatically formed that allows you to view situations from an outside perspective and resolve any conflicts.

Discover Yourself Anew

In the Kaizen method, two elements of your mind play a key role in creating a lasting positive impact on your self-image – gratitude and service. The perfection of each day is to have done something good for another person – even if it's just wishing your cashier a good day while shopping. As Mother Teresa once put it:

> *"Never let anyone come to you*
> *without letting them go better or happier."*

Interacting positively with those around you instinctively trains you to open your mindset to the world. It never hurt anyone to be polite and make others feel good. The thanks you receive will warm your heart and relieve all tension in your soul. Also, start being grateful for even the smallest of things like the sunshine, beautiful moments, enough food and a bed to sleep in, and even for every single breath you are allowed to take in the world.

Grateful people are happier per se. Their mind is balanced. In this context, gratitude can be interpreted as an expression of meaningfulness and personal fulfillment. In modern society, everything is open to us as a matter of course:

- We are hungry and can satisfy it directly.

- We are bored and the TV distracts us directly from our boredom.

- We don't know something and can get the necessary information on the internet within seconds.

These are just a few examples that illustrate how we can get almost everything directly in our world. However, it is precisely because of this self-evidence that makes it particularly difficult for us to feel genuine gratitude. Just think about how often one is haunted by the thought that only one thing is missing to reach happiness: a house, a partner, summer, or whatever personal life goal one appears to be pursuing. But as soon as we possess it, we are caught in the same rut again after a short while. We once again take it for granted and seek happiness in places other than ourselves. Those who obsessively pursue their happiness miss the chance to be truly happy and be grateful for everything that life has already given them.

While we keep ourselves trapped in the past or our future, such as mourning over what we have lost or how we longingly wish for an event, we lose sight of what is essential – the present. No matter how many plans you make, you cannot completely choose your destiny. Your life runs from now on. You can freely choose things, such as your diet, environment, furnishings, profession, behavior, or even how you deal with setbacks. Far from that, however, there are arbitrary things like the weather, chance encounters, or conditions in other countries over which you have little control. We can get angry about them and get caught up in our powerlessness or we can shift our focus to the positive things. Take your chance to enjoy and appreciate the small moments. When it's raining, it's the perfect opportunity to snuggle up comfortably on the sofa with some fantastic literature and to give your mind a little rest.

Gratitude, reflecting on ourselves (an essential activity), and the desire to make others happy are things that put you in good spirits. Happy people take life as it comes and find something positive in every moment. They move forward with serenity, mindfulness, and joy, which open up a vast range of action. Their eyes always remain open to new things and experiences. However, they never lose sight of who they are, what they value, and what they like.

There are steps one can take to feel more grateful and improve their own life. To do this, it is necessary to first detach yourself from the thought that material possessions would make you happy. There may be a material thing that is important for your personal quality of life, but it's never the thing that makes you happy because that's something only you can do. The small thrill that a new object gives you will pass within a few hours. The happiness of inner peace, on the other hand, lasts forever. These three helpful methods will help you cultivate gratitude:

1. Each evening, write down three things for which you are grateful.

2. Look for the positive in every predicament.

3. Imagine worst-case scenarios to refine your perspective on your own possibilities.

Try to find your happiness, too, and be thankful for everything that is open to you. The mindfulness exercise in the first chapter helps you change the way you think and develop a positive, open mindset.

Valuable Tips for Continuous Improvement

Personal or professional changes trigger our fears because we enter unfamiliar territory and worry about relinquishing control. At the same time, change brings a lot of good. Start being positive and hopeful! Look at change as a chance to grow and learn. This is not about huge changes but about the small moments and your daily successes. Be intentional about it, and look for new ideas for goals, desired behaviors, and personal well-being. Through the Kaizen method, you can begin to put your fears of change aside and any obstacles on your path that are stopping you from reaching your goal.

Referring back to the information in this book, you will begin to raise your awareness and reap the great benefits of a conscious and mindful lifestyle. You sharpen your senses and enjoy every moment to the fullest. You feel, smell, hear, see and taste more intensely, and you finally recognize the beauty in everyday things. Now, before I let you out of this book, I'll give you ten tips on your way that will help you lead a conscious and happy life:

- Take short breaks every day to give your mind and body a break. Meditate, go for a walk, have a cup of tea, talk to your loved ones, or read an enriching book to have the strength for every challenge.

- Do things you love regularly. To do this, you should even schedule longer breaks every now and then, which is exclusively about your needs. Actively plan activities that fill your heart, give you strength, and add the necessary sparkle to your life.

- Start consuming the media actively and consciously. Filter out the information that is important to you, educates you, or makes you feel positive.

- Pay attention to your body once a day. What feelings, pains, needs, or tensions do you notice? Is your body warm or cold? Are you hungry, full, or thirsty?

- Feel your entire environment with all your senses. Now and then, throughout the day, consciously concentrate on everything that is happening around you. What do you smell? What do you hear? What colors and shapes do you perceive?

- Consciously observe your thoughts without judging them or fighting against them.

- Try your hand at the most mundane actions repeatedly, eventually mastering them.

- Eliminate your inner chaos through outer order. At the end of your life, what matters is not what you own but what you have experienced. Reduce your material possessions to the essential things that you actually need or that enrich your life. Sort out all superfluous things and sell or donate them. It is much easier to breathe in a free, tidy space.

- Use a consumption diary in which you note down all your purchases. This will help you keep track of your spending and save a lot of money that you can invest in nice activities, like a vacation at the seaside.

- Stress is a real happiness killer. You should plan enough time for every task – even for breakfast. Ideally, you should set up a small buffer so you can experience the day calmly and happily.

- Perform even the most minor activities consciously! If you answer your e-mails while eating, it is much more difficult for you to focus on what is important. Fill every moment with gratitude, joy, pleasure, and love. Only in this way will you regain the necessary body awareness that serves as a compass for your entire life.

Afterword

It may be difficult for you to figure out where to start and what to do next because of the abundance of information. Keep in mind that you are not alone in this! Society encourages people to live an unhealthy life filled with bad behavior patterns. Break free from this and remember that no master ever fell from the sky. Start small, and focus on the essentials:

Where are your personal priorities?

Find out what a happy life means to you and continuously grow in small steps. Practice mindfulness and start to feel! Feel the love and beauty of every moment just by reflecting on what is most important: the present. Be grateful for everything that nature and your destiny have given you and all they have in store for you in the future.

Get started today using one of the many methods! Take advantage of the euphoria you get in the beginning. I am sure that you will feel a significant change in your inner emotional world in no time. Do you ever feel lost? Then don't be afraid to take another look at this book. Find new inspiration right away for the next steps, the world is open to you!

With that in mind, I now leave you to a self-determined and happy new you.

Thank you very much for your trust and attention. I wish you much success and peace of mind on your personal life path!

Resources and Further Reading

Allen, J. (2003). As a man thinketh. Simon & Schuster.

Ben-Shahar, T. (2007). Happier: Learn the secrets to daily joy and lasting fulfillment. McGraw-Hill.

Brown, B. (2012). Daring greatly: How the courage to be vulnerable transforms the way we live, love, parent, and lead. Avery.

Dweck, C. S. (2006). Mindset: The new psychology of success. Random House.

Frankl, V. E. (2006). Man's search for meaning. Beacon Press.

Kabat-Zinn, J. (1994). Wherever you go, there you are: Mindfulness meditation in everyday life. Hyperion.

Langer, E. J. (1989). Mindfulness. Addison-Wesley.

Peale, N. V. (2003). The power of positive thinking. Touchstone.

Ruettiger, R., & Sisti, A. (2003). Rudy's insights for winning in life. HCI.

Seligman, M. E. P. (2002). Authentic happiness: Using the new positive psychology to realize your potential for lasting fulfillment. Free Press.

Made in United States
Troutdale, OR
09/14/2023

12895676R00076